THE RECANTATION
OF GALILEO GALILEI

*the text of this book is printed
on 100% recycled paper*

Other Dramatic Works by Eric Bentley

ORPHEUS IN THE UNDERWORLD (*libretto, Program Publishing Company, 1956*)

A TIME TO DIE *and* A TIME TO LIVE (*two plays, Grove Press, 1970*)

THE RED WHITE AND BLACK (*a "political demonstration," Liberation, 1970*)

ARE YOU NOW OR HAVE YOU EVER BEEN (*documentary drama, Harper and Row, 1972*)

The engraving on the title page, signed P. Féras and E. Roevens, was made on the occasion of the première of the drama *Galilée* by François Ponsard at the Comédie Française, March 6, 1867. It records the final image in the play, the recantation. (*Bibliothèque de l'Arsenal*)

Scenes from History Perhaps

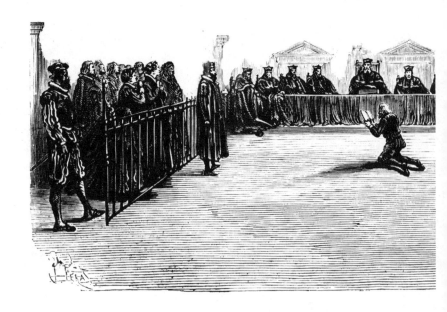

THE RECANTATION OF GALILEO GALILEI

Eric Bentley

HARPER COLOPHON BOOKS
HARPER & ROW, PUBLISHERS
New York, Evanston, San Francisco, London

Grateful acknowledgement is made to *The New York Times* for permission to reprint "Vatican May Lift Censure of Galileo." Copyright © 1968 by The New York Times Company.

THE RECANTATION OF GALILEO GALILEI. Copyright © 1972 by Eric Bentley. All rights reserved. Printed in the United States of America. No part of this book may be used or reproduced in any manner without written permission except in the case of brief quotations embodied in critical articles and reviews. For information address Harper & Row, Publishers, Inc., 10 East 53rd Street, New York, N.Y. 10022. Published simultaneously in Canada by Fitzhenry & Whiteside Limited, Toronto. Enquiries about performance rights should be addressed to Eric Bentley, c/o Cynthia Merman, Harper & Row, 10 East 53rd Street, New York, N.Y. 10022.

First HARPER COLOPHON edition published 1972.

LIBRARY OF CONGRESS CATALOG CARD NUMBER: 72-6398

STANDARD BOOK NUMBER: 06-090286-8

"It is considered that Oppenheimer is deeply concerned with gaining a worldwide reputation as a scientist and a place in history as a result of the [Manhattan Project]. It is also believed that the Army is in the position of being able to allow him to do so or to destroy his name, reputation, and career, if it should choose to do so. Such a possibility, if strongly presented to him, would possibly give him a different view of his position with respect to the Army. . . ."

—Memorandum of a United States security agent
in the dossier of J. Robert Oppenheimer, 1943

"If all you had to do to rid yourself of the new ideas was to stop the mouth of one person, that might be easy, but you would have to forbid all men to look at the sky lest they see how Mars and Venus are behaving. Even to build a wall around the thinkers is not always easy, for the true philosopher will not stay on the ground: he flies, like the eagle, even if, like the eagle, he must fly alone. Who can set bounds to the mind of man? . . . But I had rather all my books were burned, I had rather tear out my right eye, than lend comfort to the enemies of my church and endanger my immortal soul."

—Galileo Galilei, 1613

For Friedrich Heer
a good Catholic who has made the real recantation

"You cain't keep the world from movering around
Or stop old Nat Turner from gaining ground."

Contents

Acknowledgments

Though what follows is but "play" (*a* play, if you insist) and is made up of "imaginary conversations" I want to acknowledge the generous help I have received from the great Galileo scholar, Stillman Drake. If I embroidered upon facts, I was never uninterested in learning more about what the facts were and to what extent they have been verified. Drake answered all questions, general or picayune, unstintingly. For editorial work on the pictures I am indebted to Cynthia Merman and Robert Silberman.

Spring 1972   E. B.

Portrait of Galileo by Justus Sustermans, painted in 1635—two years after
the recantation—and today in the Uffizi Gallery, Florence. (*Bettmann
Archive*)

Prologue

June 22, 1633. In the great hall of the Convent of Santa Maria Sopra Minerva in Rome, a man in a penitential shirt is on his knees before the Congregation of the Holy Office. A Bible on the stone floor beside him, he reads from a scroll as follows:

I, GALILEO GALILEI, DO NOW, WITH A SINCERE HEART AND UNFEIGNED FAITH, ABJURE, DETEST, AND CURSE THE HERETICAL BELIEF THAT THE EARTH MOVES AROUND THE SUN, AND TAKE MY OATH THAT NEVER AGAIN WILL I SPEAK, WRITE, OR OTHERWISE ASSERT ANYTHING THAT MIGHT LEND PLAUSIBILITY TO THIS BELIEF. SHOULD ANYONE SUSPECTED OF SUBSCRIBING TO THIS HERETICAL BELIEF BE KNOWN TO ME, I SHALL DENOUNCE HIM TO THIS HOLY OFFICE IN ROME OR TO THE INQUISITOR IN WHATSOEVER PLACE I SHALL BE, SO HELP ME GOD AND THIS HOLY BOOK.

Galileo's home in Padua as photographed by Stillman Drake.

Scene One

ON REVOLUTIONS

The city of Padua in the Republic of Venice. A room in the home of Galileo Galilei, professor of mathematics at the University of Padua. Books, scientific apparatus. A huge volume is on a special reading stand in the middle of the room. Sunday evening. Someone is playing a lute on the floor above. After a few moments there comes a quiet knocking at the door. A girl in her early teens crosses the room to answer it. She admits a young man, evidently a student, about eighteen years old.

STUDENT. Is Professor Galilei at home?

GIRL. He's not expecting you, is he?

STUDENT. He said to come over any evening soon around nine.

GIRL. This is Sunday. And he has people coming.

STUDENT, *starting to leave.* I'll try again tomorrow then. You're not his daughter, are you?

GIRL. Oh, yes.

STUDENT. Your name's Virginia, isn't it?

GIRL. Yes.

STUDENT. Mine's Castelli. Benedetto Castelli.

VIRGINIA. One of father's students?

CASTELLI. Yes. He told us he needed a student assistant. I'm applying for the job.

VIRGINIA. Well, look, if you want to wait, I can put you over here. *She indicates another room.* He may find a minute for you later. Do you have something to read?

CASTELLI. Yes, yes. *The music has continued.* Is that *him* playing?

VIRGINIA. Yes. He always plays on "exciting occasions."

But the music is serene.

3

CASTELLI. He doesn't sound excited.

VIRGINIA. He is, though. He plays to calm himself down.

CASTELLI. What's he excited *about?*

Another knock at the door, a less timid one this time.

VIRGINIA. Oh dear, they're here already!

CASTELLI. Is he having a party tonight?

VIRGINIA. His weekly meeting with Signor Sagredo and Father Sarpi. Do you know them?

CASTELLI. Everyone knows Father Sarpi—by reputation.

VIRGINIA. He's not at all the way people say—

CASTELLI. Dangerous? He teaches at the university and most of the faculty think he's a dangerous nut. Who's Sagredo?

VIRGINIA. A fine gentleman. With a huge villa and four dozen servants. Knows all about science too—

A slightly more insistent knock. Virginia by now has placed Castelli where he can stay and read—in the next room—and she is back at the outer door. A middle-aged priest enters, wiry, intense, virile, and with a twinkle in his eye. When he hugs Virginia, one senses that she is still an even smaller girl to him.

SARPI. Virginia, my dear!

VIRGINIA. Sorry to take so long! There's a student here waiting to see daddy.

SARPI, *with the ease of a family friend.* How's the convent school?

VIRGINIA. Oh, I love it, Father. I . . . think I may stay in the convent . . . *after* school.

SARPI, *quite surprised.* You want to be a nun? Really?

VIRGINIA. You're not shocked, are you, and you a priest?

SARPI. The name Galilei would then signify the union of science and religion: a pretty thought. But you have to be sure our church and you can get along together.

VIRGINIA. Oh, I hope the church can put up with me!

SARPI. The question sometimes is if we can put up with it, my dear Virginia.

Another knock at the door.

VIRGINIA. That'll be Signor Sagredo.

She hurries to the door. The man she admits is a thirty-year-old Venetian who combines the hauteur of an aristocracy with the sophistication of an intelligentsia. A little spoiled but intelligent enough to know it, Sagredo treats himself, as well as others, with a touch of irony.

SAGREDO. Well, how's my god-daughter? *He picks her up and kisses her.* I saw your mother yesterday. With your step-father—

VIRGINIA. Oh! How is she?

SAGREDO. She likes being married for a change. She likes living with a non-genius, for a change, too, eh, Sarpi? *He shakes hands with Sarpi.*

SARPI. Certainly the genius upstairs is glad he never got married at all. . . .

Evidently Galileo was coming downstairs when this was said since his voice is heard answering it before he actually appears.

VOICE OF GALILEO. Would *you* like to get married, Sarpi? I thought you priests favored celibacy.

Galileo enters now with a telescope in his hand. The man we thus encounter is at first indistinguishable from many another brilliant academician in early middle age. We become aware of the high voltage of his personality only as he talks or paces the room. Even then it may only be nervousness, not brilliance, that reveals itself. His manner soon informs us that he is one who tends to brush obstacles aside and get on with the job, a propensity which friendly observers see as singleness of purpose or even purity, yet which the less friendly can see, with equal reason, as impatience or ruthlessness. He recites playfully:

> The world is full of woes, I've heard it said
> Then why shouldst thou refuse to get thee wed?
> To eat dry meat, or not to eat at all,
> Shiver in June, or stifle in the fall
> Sit at a play and yet not see a thing
> Or all day dance attendance on a king:
> The world is full of woes, I've heard it said
> But of all these, the worst is—to be wed.

SAGREDO. Enter Galileo, quoting Ariosto.

GALILEO. A yet profaner spirit, my dear Sagredo.

SARPI. Francisco Berni, poet of the Roman taverns and whorehouses.

GALILEO. The Vatican is right, Father Sarpi, the Jesuits are right: you are a dangerous fellow, you keep bad company, *he points at Sagredo and himself,* you even read the wrong poets. How are you both? *He shows them where to sit, but they remain standing.*

VIRGINIA. A student came, father. I put him in the study. Wants to be your assistant.

GALILEO. He'll have to wait. For, gentlemen, I come before you tonight with a proposal of some weight. You can run along, little lady. *He gives his daughter a hug and packs her off.*

SAGREDO. What's that you've got there? *He points at the telescope, which is a very primitive affair, little more than the simplest of tubes.*

GALILEO. This? Oh, I use it as an effective prop. So one of my students will come up with a drawing: "Galileo at the blackboard, pointer in hand." *He holds the telescope like a pointer.*

SARPI. But it's a tube.

GALILEO. Yes. I'm at my old game of stealing other people's ideas.

SAGREDO. Who invented the tube?

GALILEO. I haven't the slightest idea. I bought it in a toy shop. The shopman said the kids love it. A new type of magnifying glass, using two lenses instead of one. The tube is just somewhere to put the lenses.

SAGREDO. What use is it?

SARPI. How much does it magnify?

GALILEO. You two do know the right questions to ask, don't you? But can we shelve this?

SARPI. Yes, yes. Let's hear your proposal.

GALILEO. Sit down, gentlemen. *He takes the big book from the stand, and sits at the end of a table. They sit at his left and right hand.* To cut a long story short, we three have been reading this together now for—how may years, is it?

SAGREDO. Five or six.

SARPI. More.

GALILEO, *reading the title off the cover.* On Revolutions by Niklaus Copernicus. And its main idea is the greatest revolution of them all.

SAGREDO. Its main idea is worth all the books of the Bible put together.

SARPI. Ts, ts, ts, Sagredo: the Holy Bible will continue to have its uses!

SAGREDO. Yet your enthusiasm for Copernicus is as great as mine.

SARPI. Greater.

GALILEO. I'm very pleased by these interruptions, gentlemen. Enthusiasm is my theme tonight. And delight. And confidence. Now that we have absorbed this very great conception, now that we comprehend it, above all now that we have agreed together that it is *true*, a gratifying and thrilling conclusion awaits us: we must give this gospel, these tidings of great joy, to the world.

SAGREDO. Make a public announcement?

SARPI. With our names on it?

GALILEO. "The great vision of Copernicus is hereby endorsed by Galilei, Sarpi, and Sagredo." Yes.

SARPI. You're convinced the time is ripe?

GALILEO. Overripe. Copernicus wrote his book more than half a century ago. It has been read from one end of Christendom to the other. In Protestant Germany, our colleague Kepler has been able to come out for it; nothing has happened to him; and now he challenges me, in the name of science, to do the same in Catholic Italy. I'm not even the first: Giordano Bruno has already come out for it—

SAGREDO. I'm surprised to hear you use *that* argument.

GALILEO. Why?

SARPI, *with a glance at Sagredo.* Well, you know where Bruno now is, don't you?

GALILEO. No.

SAGREDO. On trial before the Inquisition in Rome.

GALILEO. But he was here just the other day! And the Venetian Republic doesn't extradite anyone. Especially not on the Inquisition's behalf.

SARPI. The Inquisition had him kidnapped.

GALILEO. Sarpi, your idea of the Inquisition comes straight from Protestant London.

SAGREDO. But Sarpi's right.

GALILEO. I don't believe it. But let's not quarrel. Where was I? Yes, I was saying the Italian people are now ready for our new view of things.

SAGREDO. I see no grounds for believing that.

SARPI. Our own students, even the most brilliant, are not yet ready.

GALILEO. I beg leave to test that remark.

SAGREDO. What?

SARPI. Here and now? How is that possible?

GALILEO. One moment. *He strides to the doorway of the room where Castelli is reading. To Castelli.* Hello. What's your name, by the way?

CASTELLI. Castelli.

GALILEO. Gentlemen, this is Castelli, a student of mine. *They murmur a greeting.* May we use you as a guinea pig?

CASTELLI. I don't quite understand.

GALILEO. Well, we want to get a student reaction to . . . something.

CASTELLI. Oh. Go right ahead.

GALILEO. Have you attended my lectures on the structure of the universe?

CASTELLI. Oh yes, sir.

GALILEO. What view did I set forth?

CASTELLI. That of Ptolemy: cycles and epicycles, the earth in the center, the sun revolving around it, the spheres. . . .

GALILEO. What other view is there?

CASTELLI. Oh, Giordano Bruno has all *sorts* of notions. . . .

GALILEO. Bruno. Who else?

CASTELLI. I don't know.

GALILEO. Copernicus. My question to you is: should I endorse him?

CASTELLI. Would that mean you don't believe what you teach in your lectures?

GALILEO. That might follow, mightn't it?

CASTELLI. What *is* the new view?

GALILEO. Hear that, Sagredo? Sarpi? *Sancta simplicitas!* Well, young man, the new view is the opposite of the old view. The earth is *not* in the center and is *not* stationary. It moves. Will your mind receive that notion? If not, you're out of luck, because the earth moves twice over: once by rotation about its own axis and again by revolution about the sun.

CASTELLI. That's . . . incredible.

SAGREDO, *an "I told you so."* Aha!

CASTELLI. It's contrary to fact!

Sarpi turns with a smile to Galileo. Galileo raises his hand.

GALILEO. Wait a minute, Sarpi. *To Castelli. Is* it contrary to fact?

CASTELLI. You ask me seriously? After your own lectures, which were so inspiring. . . . Oh, but then you don't believe your own lectures, do you? I'm confused.

GALILEO. You have the right to be. We three oldsters are only just emerging from that confusion. Let me ease the strain with an *if. If* this view were true, what difference would it make?

CASTELLI. We would have to . . . see *everything* differently, wouldn't we?

GALILEO. Go on.

CASTELLI. We'd have to see the earth as . . . a sort of *flying machine,* such as Leonardo da Vinci imagined. We'd have to see ourselves as *voyagers* on a flying machine, voyagers through space!

GALILEO. That's very good, I wish *I'd* said that. May I remove the *if?*

CASTELLI. The *if?*

GALILEO. I said *if* the Copernican view were true. It *is* true, so help me God! As for my lectures, Castelli, well, I lead a double life. On weekdays, I'm a disciple of Ptolemy. On Sunday evenings, when I meet with Sarpi and Sagredo, I say a black mass, cook a spiritual minestrone in a witches' cauldron, and whisper a magic incantation that makes my faculty colleagues toss uneasily in their beds: *the earth revolves, the sun stands still.*

CASTELLI. Can I study the new view, sir?

GALILEO. Hear that, gentlemen? Now, Signor Castelli, would you do something for me? Go out and get the latest news sheets on the Square. Ask especially for news of Giordano Bruno. *Castelli leaves the house.* He wants to study the new view.

SARPI, *laughing.* This is one student.

SAGREDO. And one that likes you.

GALILEO. All right. Was this one student, drawn from the large class of young people that likes me, ready for the news?

SARPI. He certainly was.

SAGREDO. I enjoyed every moment of it: *I'd* like to have him as a student.

9

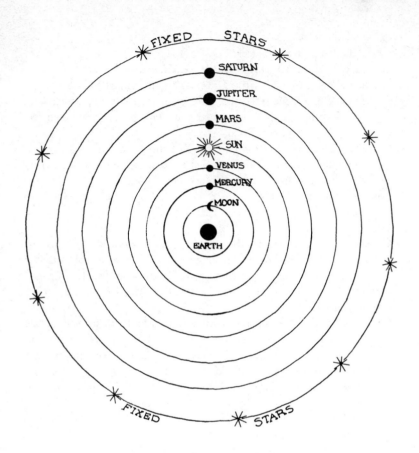

THE SYSTEM OF THE WORLD IN
BROAD OUTLINES ACCORDING TO
PTOLEMY

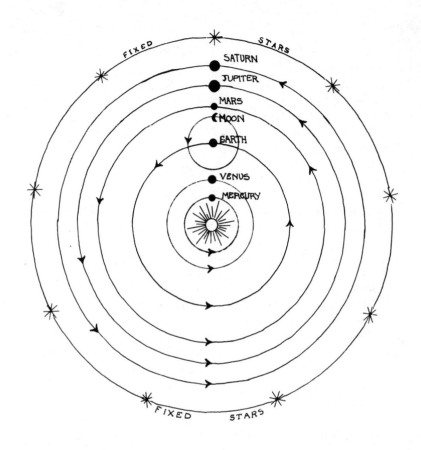

THE SYSTEM OF THE WORLD IN
BROAD OUTLINES ACCORDING TO
COPERNICUS

GALILEO. Well then?

SARPI. Well, Sagredo, we are not conceding there are no risks. But shall we take a chance?

SAGREDO. And cry, *Fiat justitia, ruat coelum?* I have misgivings.

Noise of opening door. Castelli rushes in.

CASTELLI. The news is terrible, sir!

GALILEO. Yes? What then?

CASTELLI. Giordano Bruno is *dead.*

SARPI, *jumping up.* He was—

SAGREDO, *ditto.* Executed?

SARPI, *seizing the news sheet, and reading from it.* ". . . taken from his prison in the Tower of Nona to the Campo dei Fiori, he was there stripped naked, bound to a stake, and burned alive."

SAGREDO, *grabbing the sheet from Sarpi.* "Two Dominicans and two Jesuits showed him his errors yet he stubbornly held onto his vainglorious fantasies. One of the Jesuits, thinking he might repent, held up the image of Jesus before him on a pole, but Bruno turned his face away, weeping wildly. The sentence was then read by the Lord Cardinal Bellarmine."

SARPI. The most important Jesuit of them all. Did Bruno say anything?

SAGREDO, *scanning the sheet.* Yes. "He said, 'Better a spirited death than a craven life.' At this, Bellarmine called on him in a loud voice to repent but Bruno answered, 'Clearly you fear me more than I you.' "

Pause.

GALILEO. Couldn't there be some mistake? These news sheet editors—

SARPI. To print this—if it was a lie—would be more than any editor's life was worth.

GALILEO. It's just too awful. I don't understand.

SARPI. No one understands.

SAGREDO. Yet this is how things are.

SARPI. And it's good we've been reminded—in time.

SAGREDO. That's true. We were on the brink of a colossal blunder.

GALILEO. Huh?

SAGREDO. To make your announcement now is to ask for what Bruno got.

SARPI. We were crazy to even consider it. I've been asking myself for years if I shouldn't drop these scientific studies altogether and concentrate on the prior necessity.

GALILEO. Which is?

SARPI. To restore this church of ours to health. Well, now I know. From now on, just that must be my mission.

GALILEO. You are unfair. If Bellarmine agreed to . . . this, he had his reasons. . . . I *hate* to hear you talk against our church!

SARPI. The hierarchy is not the church.

GALILEO, *petulantly*. And what is? You?

SARPI, *calmly*. Yes. And you. Wherever two or three are gathered. All.

GALILEO, *sarcastically*. Even Protestants, I suppose?

SARPI. Even Jews. Moslems. . . . All. That is my vision. Our vision. The vision of a church that is *really* catholic.

SAGREDO. It is staggering.

Pause.

GALILEO. No more Sunday evenings anyway. From now on you will be a professional agitator, huh? What about you, Sagredo?

SAGREDO. Oh, I'll live on my estates. And never venture outside this Republic of Venice. Don't worry about me. What will *you* do?

SARPI. You will *not* make that announcement.

GALILEO. No. I'll be silent, don't worry. For a while.

SAGREDO. Forever, if you ask my advice.

GALILEO. No. One day I will have physical evidence. The Copernican theory mustn't be something that needs endorsement, even mine. It must be independent of all authority, even mine.

SAGREDO. Is that going to be possible?

GALILEO. A true proposition, in physical science, is one for which there is physical evidence.

SAGREDO. In principle, yes, but can you find any? Copernicus didn't manage it. Bruno didn't manage it.

SARPI. The trouble being that the heavens—the infinite spaces about us— are inaccessible.

SAGREDO. We cannot sail to the moon!

GALILEO, *slowly*. If we cannot—as yet—sail to the moon, can we make the moon sail to us?

13

SAGREDO. Magic, eh?

GALILEO. Well then, *seem* to sail to us. Can we strengthen our eyesight until it penetrates space. Better spectacles, better magnifying glasses. . . .

He picks up the telescope again.

SAGREDO. All right: go ahead and perfect that tube till you can see all the secrets of the skies through it!

GALILEO. Hm? Is that an idea of yours I'm allowed to steal?

SAGREDO. For what little it's worth.

SARPI. Galileo's ideas were seldom worth much to those he stole them from.

SAGREDO. Will you work on it then?

GALILEO. I shall work on this idea and a hundred others. The evidence is there: I have only to find it.

SAGREDO. When you have it, will it turn the trick?

GALILEO. If the earth is moving, it won't grind to a halt to satisfy the Padua faculty.

SAGREDO. Well, let me know if you ever do find this evidence. I can always be dragged off my vineyards.

SARPI. Let *me* know too, Galileo. I can always be dragged off my soapbox.

GALILEO. So you're both leaving me. My, it's worse than the night I parted from Virginia's mother! But I won't say goodbye, it's just *arrivederci,* isn't it? I am going to find this evidence and hale you over here if I have to come for you into the very dungeons of the Inquisition.

SAGREDO. Venice for the Venetians! You can postpone all thoughts of the Inquisition till you leave these parts, which I trust will be never. Goodbye.

SARPI. Goodbye, dear friend. *They embrace.* I fear for you: but you must do what you must do. I wish you the pagans' luck and our own God's care. You will need both.

Sarpi and Sagredo leave.

GALILEO. Well, young man, it was you who brought the fateful news of Bruno's death. Are you also the last to leave me?

CASTELLI. I don't want to leave you, Professor.

GALILEO. It's a mouthful, though, isn't it? A new universe? And a burning at the stake in prospect? *Pause.* Do you know what you want, Castelli?

CASTELLI. I want to be your assistant, Professor.

GALILEO. Hm. Know anything about optics?

CASTELLI. No.

GALILEO. Nor do I. Maybe we can learn it together?

CASTELLI. Am I hired, then?

GALILEO, *nodding.* Bring me everything the library has on optics.

Galileo's telescope as preserved in the observatory at Arcetri, the village near Florence where Galileo spent his last years. (*Bettmann Archive*)

Scene Two

THE TELESCOPE

The same room, but time has passed. Evening. The telescope, set up on a stand, now dominates one side of the room. Galileo is peering through it; Castelli sits ready to take notes. No dialogue for a while. Only the grunts of Galileo as he moves the instrument and changes the field of vision. A relaxed atmosphere: both men are happy. Then a knock at the door.

GALILEO. Not to be disturbed till 10 o'clock! Go away!

VIRGINIA'S VOICE. It's me, daddy. There's mail for you.

GALILEO. Not interested! The committee's coming!

VIRGINIA. But this is special. From foreign parts. One letter has "Grand Duke of Tuscany" on the envelope!

GALILEO. Oh, it does? Excuse me a minute, Castelli.

He opens the door to Virginia.

So you call Florence foreign parts, eh?

He has opened one letter. He lets out a yell of triumph.

Hey! Castelli! He says he will!

CASTELLI. Who will what, maestro?

GALILEO. The grand duke has been deluging me with offers for several years. Double my Padua salary. Half the teaching load. So I kept leading him on. Asked him in my last if he would come out for the new view of the universe, should I take the job. He now says he would!

CASTELLI. Does he know what's involved?

GALILEO. I'm not going to Florence anyway. After the meeting this morning, we shall have the endorsement of the University of Padua. That will suffice.

Knock at the door.

VIRGINIA. They're early.

GALILEO. No, no, that will be Sarpi and Sagredo. I asked them to come first. Let them in, Virginia. *She does.* Sarpi! Sagredo! *They embrace.*

SARPI. Galileo!

SAGREDO. You haven't changed a bit.

GALILEO. Well, old friends, you asked to be brought back on The Day: this is The Day. And that's the offending party. *He points to the telescope.* No words. Point that thing at the sky and tell me what you see. Or rather, tell yourselves what you see, since I know.
He leaves Sarpi and Sagredo to experiment with the telescope, while he moves over to the other side of the room. What was the other letter, Virginia?

VIRGINIA. Here.

GALILEO. Ah! This one really is from foreign parts, Austria anyway, and I recognize the handwriting. It's Herr Kepler's. I sent him one of my telescopes. Would you like to read it to me?

VIRGINIA, *taking it back.* "O spy glass, instrument of much knowledge, more precious than any scepter, is not he who holds thee in his hand made king and overlord of the works of God?" I don't quite get it.

GALILEO, *pacing to and fro in what we shall come to regard as a characteristic manner, nervous yet purposeful.* Nature is the work of God, and Nature isn't just the garden and the vineyard opposite and the cypresses on the ridge beyond, it's the whole green earth with the blue air around it and the white clouds overhead, and it's more again than these: it is the sun and moon and stars and the infinite silent spaces.

VIRGINIA. The same as the Bible: "the heavens declare the glory of God."

GALILEO. The same as the Bible.
From the other side of the room.

SAGREDO. That's Jupiter all right, but what's going on all around?

SARPI. I thought there were specks on the lens but now I've cleaned it.

SAGREDO. They are objects. In the sky. Near Jupiter.

SARPI. Let me look again.
Back to Galileo and Virginia.

VIRGINIA, *still reading.*

"All that is overhead, the mighty orbs
With all their motions Thou dost subjugate
To man's intelligence."

GALILEO. The Bible says that too, remember?

VIRGINIA. The eighth Psalm. "When I consider Thy heavens, the work of Thy fingers, the moon and the stars, which Thou hast ordained. . . ."

GALILEO. "Thou madest him to have dominion over the works of Thy hands."

VIRGINIA. So Herr Kepler thinks you're a god.

GALILEO. No, not at all—

VIRGINIA. I used to think you were a god myself. The Greek kind. The kind that comes down from Mount Olympus to make a conquest of the ladies.

GALILEO. And you want to be a nun? Why, I'll report you to the Jesuits, and they'll burn you as a heretic.

VIRGINIA. The Jesuits have been expelled from Venice.

GALILEO. You know everything, don't you? Except the interpretation of the Bible. In "Thou madest him to have dominion," "Thou" is God, "him" is man. . . .
Back to Sagredo and Sarpi.

SARPI. *Four* objects. Jupiter is surrounded by four.. . . .

SAGREDO. Just a minute. Let me take another look. *He puts his eye to the telescope.* How do you know which is Jupiter?

SARPI. It's bigger.

SAGREDO. Right. It's bigger. But, Sarpi, that is the *only* difference.

SARPI. How *can* it be the only difference? That would be to say that . . . let me look again.
Galileo begins to listen to his friends' conversation.

VIRGINIA. But the man that "has dominion" is you—

GALILEO. Shh!

SARPI, *very slowly and distinctly, with amazement.* The four specks are also planets.

SAGREDO. Let me look.

GALILEO. Listen to this, Virginia.

SAGREDO. There are four planets around Jupiter.

SARPI. Four planets never before beheld by the eye of man!

GALILEO. Well, how is that, gentlemen, for a beginning? The universe has other secrets up its sleeve, several of which I am about to divulge to the Faculty Committee on the Sciences.

SARPI. You have physical evidence for the whole Copernican theory?

GALILEO. Enough.

SARPI. I can't wait to hear it.

SAGREDO. The faculty committee is on its way here? What do you hope to get out of *them?*

GALILEO. See for yourselves. Getting this committee to come out here was no small matter. I gave it all I had. Dean Bruciano was here already, looked through the telescope at the surrounding landscape, and became an ally. He is bringing the group in his coach tonight. *Knocking at the door.* My God, here they are. Virginia!

She goes to the door and lets in seven men. Not seven clowns. Rather, citizens of some distinction, from the viewpoint of most of whom Galileo is the clown. *Men of the world, they would not wish the world to be mocked.*

Dean Bruciano, I'd like you to meet my old friends Father Sarpi and Signor Sagredo. My daughter Virginia and my assistant Castelli you already know. *Bowing on all sides.*

SCHOLAR 1, *evidently Dean Bruciano.* Rizzi, Seggizi, LoVecchio, Guarini, Lorini, Scheiner. *Each of these bows as his name is spoken.*

GALILEO. You are seven. Isn't it a committee of nine?

SCHOLAR 1. Oh, um, yes, Sforza and Magrini were, um, indisposed.

GALILEO. That's too bad, they're in my field. Anyway, gentlemen, I see where your eyes are tending, that contraption is indeed the telescope. I have several others you can take away with you when you leave. Dean Bruciano has already witnessed some of the telescope's powers. As have Sarpi and Sagredo. Nevertheless, the pith and point of these proceedings have been saved for the present moment. Gentlemen, I did not invent the telescope. What I did was realize what to point it at.

SCHOLAR 2. How's that?

GALILEO. The children had been using it this way. *He places it horizontally*. They could see down the street, across country, over the sea, even through lightly curtained windows. But one evening, by a stroke of genius, I fell over it, knocked it into this position, *he places it vertically*, lay on my back to use it, and saw—

SCHOLAR 3, *a wag*. God Almighty?

GALILEO. Well, to be frank, absolutely nothing. But it gave me an idea. "I will lift up mine eyes unto the hills: from thence cometh my help." Or rather, just above the hills, thus. *He has been playing with the telescope. It now points upward but aslant*. And saw the next best thing to God, Professor Seggizi: the sun and the moon. Castelli, are both of them perfect, unblemished, crystal spheres?

CASTELLI. That's what you said in your lectures.

GALILEO. When observed through the telescope, the sun is seen to have spots on it. Not spots on the lens, Father Sarpi, spots on the sun. As for the moon, does it have a smooth, even surface?

CASTELLI. That has been the assumption.

GALILEO. Whereas actually the moon has a rugged surface, being mountainous.

SCHOLAR 3. Does the man in the moon live in a valley or on a mountain top?

GALILEO. The topic has changed now: we shall begin to think, instead, of a man *on* the moon. Lacking, of course, is the right kind of ship to sail there on. . . . Which of you is familiar with the planet Venus? Oh come, the shape of Venus has been of perennial interest to the male sex, but the shape of her namesake in the sky will astonish the human race, male and female, for, gentlemen, it keeps changing. Can the changes be accounted for?

CASTELLI. Not on the supposition that Venus revolves around the earth.

GALILEO. But on the supposition that she revolves around the sun? What did you learn in my class about Jupiter?

CASTELLI. That she shines in lone splendor.

GALILEO. Sarpi and Sagredo, when you arrived this evening the telescope was trained on Jupiter. What did you see through it?

SCHOLAR 3. Jupiter! A miracle!

GALILEO. Jupiter. And what else?

SARPI. Four other planets.

GALILEO. I call them the satellites of Jupiter. Physical evidence that Ptolemy's view of the universe was wrong. Physical evidence that Copernicus was right.

SCHOLAR 1. Now, let me get this straight, Galilei. Have you brought us here to—

GALILEO. You represent the University of Padua. This University now has the opportunity to announce to the entire civilized world a truth of majestic proportions and unbounded possibility.

SCHOLAR 1. You told me nothing of this! All I saw through that tube was landscape—

SCHOLAR 2. Galilei, like yourself I have been teaching the Ptolemaic universe for decades. D'you want me to throw away my lecture notes and go to school to you?

GALILEO. Don't you think it might do you a great deal of good? *Scholar 2 turns on his heel and leaves.* Oh dear, I've said the wrong thing. Wouldn't some of you like to look through the telescope? *Scholar 6 goes and does so.*

SCHOLAR 3, *shifting from a playful to an insolent tone.* Galilei, if I don't look through your spy-glass, it is not because I don't believe you see what you say you see. That, however, is no proof that it is there. The overthirsty man sees extra oases in the desert; the over-curious man sees extra stars in the sky.

GALILEO. Can a scientist be *over* curious?

SCHOLAR 4. He can be overambitious. What is not discovered can be invented.

GALILEO. You are imputing fraud.

SCHOLAR 5. Not necessarily, my dear Galilei. Human beings avoid deliberately deceiving others by involuntarily deceiving themselves.

GALILEO. Would you care to look through the telescope and report whether or not I have deceived myself?

SCHOLAR 5. Lorini's been looking through it for several minutes. I'm willing to take his word on what is presently visible through it.

SCHOLAR 6. I wish I knew. I was all set to see Jupiter and four little Jupiters, as Galilei suggested. There are a few things bobbing about there that *could* be planets but. . . .

GALILEO. Like other machines, the telescope may take a little getting used to. Visibility varies, the moon changes, there are differences from night to night. . . . I did not mean to imply, gentlemen, that you owed me an answer now. Take a telescope home with you. Or return and use mine some other night. I would only request that you keep an open mind.

SCHOLAR 1. Oh, but, Galilei, this is not at all what any of us bargained for. . . . You never even hinted that astrology—excuse me, astronomy—was involved. . . . I thought at most navigation, military engineering. . . . Please realize that none of us here is more than a dean. The rector would have to be consulted. And the regents. And I doubt that they would take kindly to switching universes on us.

GALILEO. Not even if they got all the credit? "Universes switched by order of rector and regents"?

SCHOLAR 1. So, finally, you mock me too, Galilei? I was shielding you from the real reason why Sforza and Magrini didn't come. Neither one of them can stand you. Sforza says you stole his ideas. Magrini feels he failed to get a promotion because you elbowed him out. Even tonight, when more might have been expected of you, you have caused Rizzi to walk out. I shall now follow him.

GALILEO. I imagine he's waiting for you in your coach. Good night!

They all leave. A long pause.

SAGREDO. Well, Galileo my friend, as I've told you before, you are incorrigible.

SARPI. You never did do anything by halves, did you?

SAGREDO. Your method, however, has the merit of leaving nothing in doubt. At least we don't have to discuss how you will mend your bridges and win the faculty over on a future occasion.

A knock at the door.

GALILEO, *going to the door himself.* Who can this be?

Reenter Scholar 7, a younger man than the others, and much less the academician. His eyes are earnest and fiery. He is gaunt.

SCHOLAR 7. I came back for one of your telescopes.

GALILEO. The coach drove off.

SCHOLAR 7. Yes, there was a slight altercation.

GALILEO. You will walk home for the sake of a telescope? A man after my own heart! And I don't even know your name.

SCHOLAR 7. Scheiner. Christopher Scheiner. Astronomy is my passion.

GALILEO. Then there is hope in Padua.

SCHEINER. I am leaving for Rome.

GALILEO. But there the Jesuits have a monopoly on science.

SCHEINER. I am joining the Jesuit order.

GALILEO. Well, young man, you don't do things by halves either, do you? *Gives him a telescope.* I shall follow your career carefully.

SCHEINER. And I yours, Professor Galilei.

Galileo lets him out.

GALILEO. Signor Scheiner is right. Padua is a provincial dump.

SAGREDO. The grass is greener on the other side of the street?

GALILEO. Where's that letter, Castelli? *Castelli supplies the letter from the grand duke.* "Finally, we shall hope on your behalf to make that announcement to the world by which the world shall learn its true relation to the universe. Signed: Cosimo de' Medici."

SAGREDO. "We shall hope." Florence hopes a lot of things. That the Vatican and the Jesuits won't be so strong. That its own Dominican preachers will be less influential. Don't you realize that the provincialism of Padua is your shield? No Jesuits. No Inquisition. No Vatican. No extradition. Leave this Republic of Venice, and you are naked among the wolves.

GALILEO. Don't you think I can take care of myself?

SAGREDO. You're too *naive,* Galileo. Supersubtle in science, in politics you are a babe in arms. Take tonight's exhibition! Good God, man, if you can't bend the Padua faculty to your will, how do you hope to fare with the Medici, the Dominicans, the Jesuits, the Holy Office, the Inquisition, and the pope? Help me, Sarpi. Help me save a great man for his own greatness. This may be our last chance. *Pause.*

GALILEO. Sarpi isn't helping.

SARPI. Sarpi is thinking. What Sagredo says is true, Galileo, but it influences you in the opposite direction. And while he was talking you made your decision. *You are going to Florence.*

GALILEO. Quite right. Is that perverse of me?

24

SARPI. Sagredo said it was *dangerous*. Your friends want you alive and free.

SAGREDO. I also said it was *futile*.

SARPI. I *cannot* help you, Sagredo. As you say, this is probably our farewell to our friend, and in this solemn hour, all I want is to feel I understood him. What do you live for, Galileo?

GALILEO. Hm? I want to get certain truths accepted.

SCARPI. Why?

GALILEO. Isn't is normal?

SARPI. Why?

GALILEO. Oh, you mean I'm vain? I'm proud?

SARPI. I want to understand you.

GALILEO. Well, certainly, there must be a big selfish element in it. Not just my desire for prestige and honors. My yearning to be released from this awful silence.

SARPI. You said years ago you lived for the day when the silence would cease. Can a man demand that?

GALILEO. The world owes him that.

SARPI. The world owes you something?

GALILEO. I'm even persuaded it's not such a bad world as you and Sagredo suppose. It not only owes, it will pay.

SARPI. *This* world? *This* church? *This* Italy?

GALILEO. *This* world, *this* church, *this* Italy.

SARPI. Suppose you prove wrong, and the world refuses to pay?

GALILEO. I hate supposing!

SARPI. On the contrary, you are a master of hypothesis.

GALILEO. Should the world refuse to pay, a man can do what Bruno did.

SAGREDO. Good God!

GALILEO. "Better a spirited death than a craven life."

SARPI. It's a beautiful answer, Sagredo. May an old priest be permitted a piece of advice on parting?

GALILEO. To this old priest everything is permitted.

SARPI. Should you ever, which God forbid, find yourself in Bruno's position, ask yourself if Bruno's response is, for you, the bravest and the . . . most appropriate. That's all. And goodbye.
He embraces Galileo.

SAGREDO. Goodbye, my friend. As a counsellor I'm no match for Father
Sarpi, but let me say this: you have most value—you will always
have most value—alive and kicking. *He embraces Galileo. Sarpi
and Sagredo leave.*
GALILEO. Virginia!
Virginia comes in.
Virginia, Castelli, this is a family council. I am going to Florence.
To Rome, first, on a visit; then to Florence, to live. As mathematician to the grand duke. Things can work out well there. I believe they will. But they may not. Some of my friends think they
will not. So, Virginia, it would be better if you took the veil here,
and stayed here. Castelli, you are almost ready to enter upon a career
as a scholar-priest, a priestly scientist. You too must stay here in the
free Republic of Venice.
CASTELLI. So I'm fired?
GALILEO. I didn't say *that.*
CASTELLI. You said it was a family council. That makes me a son—who
might prefer to cling to house and home.
GALILEO, *smiling.* Could you get a release from your priestly obligations
and work with me in Florence?
CASTELLI. I could. I must.
VIRGINIA. And I could enter a *Florentine* convent, and keep an eye
on you!
GALILEO. What? But I don't know any Florentine convents!
VIRGINIA. I do. I know *about* them. No problem!
GALILEO, *looking at her.* You're serious. You're both serious. Very
well, I reverse myself. Come to Florence, both of you. Keep an
eye on me, Virginia. But, Castelli, do either of you have any idea
what you're taking on?
CASTELLI. Do you?
GALILEO. No. *He laughs.* No! *All three laugh.* What was it Sarpi said
once? Yes: "No one goes so far as the man who doesn't know
where he's going."

The single "villa in Florence" of Scenes Three and Five represents a dramatic simplification, since Galileo actually lived in several different villas in or near Florence between 1610 and his trial in 1633. The two shown here are: the Villa delle Selve, about fifteen miles west of Florence (*photographed by Stillman Drake*) and Costa S. Giorgio, 13 (*Alinari*).

Scene Three

A. A VILLA IN FLORENCE

Florence. Galileo's villa. More lavish than the Padua house but not extravagant. Galileo stands at the window looking out at the city.

GALILEO, *softly.* Florence! Florence! *He shakes himself out of reverie and moves swiftly to the table where his papers are. Hums the tune he earlier played on the lute until a knock comes at the door which he then opens. Enter Virginia in convent dress.* Well, at long last you come to see my new home.

VIRGINIA. I'd have come long before, daddy, but you were in Rome.

GALILEO. Oh, that was centuries ago!

VIRGINIA. I wish I could have helped you move in here.

GALILEO. Let me take a look at you, Virginia. Stand back, that's right. Galileo's little nun.

VIRGINIA. I'm not a nun—yet. And you must call me Sister Maria.

GALILEO. Now how can a father remember to call his daughter his sister? I have a terrible memory.

VIRGINIA. For things you want to forget.

GALILEO. Quite. What happens when I call you Virginia?

VIRGINIA. I could ask God to forgive you.

GALILEO. He's good at that, isn't He?

VIRGINIA. Daddy!

GALILEO. What's the matter . . . Sister Maria?

VIRGINIA. Oh, you're incorr— What's that word you always use?

GALILEO. Incorrigible. But it's not my word, it's Sagredo's. He thinks the church itself is incorrigible. I disagree.

VIRGINIA. But that's how I like you.

GALILEO. You like my incorrigibility? I should report that to your father

confessor. *With a change of tone.* Are you happy . . . Sister
Maria?

VIRGINIA. Oh, yes. Especially now you're just an hour away from the
convent.

GALILEO. You still feel you'll want to stay there—for life?

VIRGINIA. The mother superior says she has great hopes. What about
you? Are *you* happy?

GALILEO. Very. My visit to Rome, my position here; it's all beyond my
fondest dreams.

VIRGINIA. Tell me about Rome.

GALILEO. Rome is a hoax. Rome is a whore. City of aesthetes and
dilettantes, parasites and time servers, spies and informers, go-
betweens and go-getters, bloodsucking lawyers and bootlicking
politicians, all varieties of prostitutes, temporal and spiritual. You
wouldn't like Rome.

VIRGINIA. But your visit. . . .

GALILEO. Oh, *I'm* a hit, the latest fad, the talk of the town, the life and
soul of every fashionable garden party, quoted and misquoted by
courtiers and courtesans, cardinals and monsignori. The pope
granted me six audiences. The bishops came and looked through
my telescope in the Pincio. Old Cardinal Bellarmine himself expressed interest, and a young cardinal called Barberini was suffi-
ciently carried away to write a poem in honor of Galileo and the
new astronomy.

VIRGINIA. You're bitter, daddy.

GALILEO. I would be if all roads led to Rome. My hopes rest now on
Florence, whose grand duke is about to make . . . well, that long-
awaited announcement.

VIRGINIA. Have you met him yet?

GALILEO. I have my first audience next week. He's been off in Leghorn,
inspecting his beloved fleet. Niccolini, his chamberlain, told me not
to worry at the postponement. Everything was well in hand.
A knock. Enter Castelli, excited.

CASTELLI. Maestro— *Seeing Virginia.* Oh, I didn't notice.

GALILEO, *smiling.* I want you to meet . . . Sister Maria.

CASTELLI. God bless you, Sister.

30

VIRGINIA. And you, Father Castelli. I was just leaving.

CASTELLI. No, please. *Actually he wants her to go.*

GALILEO. Come again soon.

VIRGINIA. I'm coming next week with some tagliatello. *To Castelli.* The sisters cook, and sell their dishes for the upkeep of the convent.

GALILEO. Their fathers get the stuff free—if they live near enough.

CASTELLI. She's going to spoil you more than ever, Galileo.

GALILEO. I hope so. *He kisses Virginia, and she leaves.* Well, what is it, Castelli? In Florence one just doesn't get excited like that.

CASTELLI. You were a child here. So now you see Florence through the rose-colored spectacles of reminiscent middle age.

GALILEO. Well! What *is* it?

CASTELLI. A preaching campaign has started. Last Sunday, ten different Dominicans preached the very same sermon. A sermon against you.

GALILEO. Sticks and stones may break my bones—

CASTELLI, *cutting in with another proverb.* "The preacher stands in the pulpit, the inquisitor sits in the pew." This morning a curiously anonymous looking fellow asked me after mass, "Excuse me, are you Father Castelli?" and turned on his heel as soon as I said yes.

GALILEO. Police spies were never very long on subtlety, were they? Anyhow, Florence is not ruled by these watchdogs of the Lord, it is ruled by a grand duke. A Medici at that.

CASTELLI. In the taverns they say Florence is ruled by a Dominican preacher.

GALILEO. Caccini. Caccini's a demagogue.

CASTELLI. A watchdog whose bite is worse than his bark. He has been seen at Inquisition headquarters lately.

GALILEO. I should worry?

CASTELLI. Next Sunday he will occupy the pulpit of Santa Maria Novella. As his text he has announced, "Why stand ye gazing toward Heaven, O . . . Galileans?" *He articulates this last word emphatically as he looks Galileo straight in the face.*

B. A WATCHDOG OF THE LORD

A Dominican preacher in his pulpit. His eyes are earnest but slightly watery and shifty. *His speech is loud but tends toward incantation; he listens to himself, and what he hears makes him sad.*

DOMINICAN. "Why stand ye gazing toward Heaven, O Galileans?" *He drinks water.* Dearly Beloved, we look up toward heaven to see there the works of God as in fact they are and always have been and as our church has found them to be. But I need not tell you, in this Florence of ours, that there are those among us—a small minority but a minority organized, ruthless, and backed by foreigners—who are encouraging another attitude. Let us call it the mathematical attitude. For what is this so-called science of mathematics? What else but the Devil's sign language? Does it not go hand in hand with astronomy, astrology, horoscopes, sorcery, and black magic? What else is a mathematician but a male witch? Even the Protestants—even the Protestants—have admitted that their great mathematician, *looking for the name in his notes,* Giovanni Keplero—alias Johann Kepler, a German, hiding out in Austria— is the son of a convicted witch. And here in this Florence of ours— well, what have they ever done in Florence, these scientists, I'd like to know, with their long hair and their noses in books and their fingers in experiments and other hocus-pocus? Take their latest attack on our beliefs and institutions. Look up with me into the heavens, look through the windows of this lovely Church of Santa Maria Novella, and what do you see? The sun. Where? There. *He points to the sun.* And where was it when you entered this church an hour ago? Was it not there? *He points to the east of the sun.* It has moved, has it not? And you know it. You know it. You are not rabble, and filth, and ignoramuses, as these so-called scientists say. You were in Florence before they crept out of their German holes, and you'll be here when they've been sent back where they came from, and you have eyes and can see. And if any of you want to know the why and the wherefore, you can come to me after the service and I'll read to you from this book, *he waves it,* and this, *ditto,*—Aristotle and Ptolemy—and I'll give you the facts of yesterday, today, and forever! *Very quiet again.* But there is an element in our midst, underground, like reptiles, like vermin, without the courage to show its face in this Christian city, in league with the Devil, and believing, not in religion, but in magic, that says we must not believe our own eyes or Aristotle or Ptolemy or Mother Church, we must believe *them!* There is a word, my children, that I do not like to use from this sacred pulpit. That word is heresy, but I use it now because I am going to end this sermon with an announcement. Each of us does what he can, is that not so? and what I have done this week is report some of these . . . heretical activities where each and everyone of us must report them as he sees them: at the headquarters of the Holy Inquisition. Then we shall see changes in Florence! Yes, for though the prime mover himself may for the present be able to hide behind, shall we say, ducal robes, behind Medicean ermine, the watchdogs of the Lord will sniff him out in the end! With your help, my children, and with the help of Him above. Glory be to the Father, and to the Son, and to the Holy Ghost, Amen. *He crosses himself.*

C. THE INVESTIGATION

An office. Quite bare. Castelli and an Inquisitor at either end of a long table. The Inquisitor is equipped with documents and a writing pad. Nothing grand about this Inquisitor: he is just a plump, cantankerous, small-time investigator, "most ignorant of what he's most assured."

CASTELLI, *spelling his name for the Inquisitor who writes it down.*
  C, A, S, T, E, L, L, I.
INQUISITOR. Italian?
CASTELLI. Yes.
INQUISITOR. Are you sure?
CASTELLI. Yes.
INQUISITOR. On both sides?
CASTELLI. Yes.

INQUISITOR. Can you prove it?

CASTELLI. Yes.

INQUISITOR. We are collecting information on Galileo Galilei. You work for him?

CASTELLI. Yes.

INQUISITOR. Why?

CASTELLI. I am interested in science.

INQUISITOR, *consulting papers.* The science taught by Galilei is based on the work of one Hibernicus, correct?

CASTELLI. Copernicus.

INQUISITOR. A Russian?

CASTELLI. A Pole.

INQUISITOR. Are you quibbling with me?

CASTELLI. It isn't a quibble. The Poles are Catholic, the Russians aren't.

INQUISITOR. Hibernicus's book is called "On Revolution." Is that a Catholic title?

CASTELLI. It's called "On Revolution*s*." Plural. Of the globe, that is.

INQUISITOR. What globe?

CASTELLI. This one.

INQUISTOR. Which one?

CASTELLI. The one we're sitting on.

INQUISITOR. Are you telling the Holy Roman Inquisition that we are sitting on a globe, and that it revolves?

CASTELLI. I am reporting that Copernicus believed this; and that he was a Pole and a Catholic.

INQUISITOR. A bad Catholic!

CASTELLI. A canon of the church. A friend of His Holiness Pope Paul III.

INQUISITOR. You were not asked for a lecture on church history. Does Professor Galilei also believe that the earth revolves around the sun?

Pause.

CASTELLI. I am not entitled to speak for Professor Galilei.

INQUISITOR. Has he not taught the opposite theory for years?

CASTELLI. I think he has.

INQUISITOR. When did he stop doing so?

CASTELLI. I couldn't say.

INQUISITOR, *writing in his book.* He has stopped doing so, but you couldn't say exactly when.

CASTELLI. I am confused now.

INQUISITOR. Is Galilei currently teaching that the earth is stationary?

CASTELLI. I couldn't say.

INQUISITOR. You said his view was based on Hibernicus. You said Hibernicus believed the earth goes round the sun. You have therefore affirmed that Galilei believes the earth goes round the sun. I'm asking you if he is currently teaching what he believes?

CASTELLI. I'm not sure.

INQUISITOR. So that Galilei is a teacher whose own pupils don't know what he is currently teaching. Or whether he is sincere, and teaches what he believes. What does he mean by saying, "God is an accident"?

CASTELLI. I don't know.

INQUISITOR. Then he did say it. You just didn't understand. How about when he pictured Our Lord as laughing?

CASTELLI. I don't recall. . . .

INQUISITOR, *making a note.* It was said but it has been forgotten. Do you recall if you tried to correct him? You are in holy orders. It would be your task to correct such a statement.

CASTELLI. No, but then—

INQUISITOR, *another note.* No attempt to correct. Does he believe in miracles?

CASTELLI, *more and more distressed.* How can I answer that question for another man?

INQUISITOR. Claiming to be a Christian, Galilei leaves it doubtful, even to his intimates, whether he accepts the miracles of Christ. Is he a bachelor?

CASTELLI. Yes.

INQUISITOR. And yet he has a daughter?

CASTELLI. Yes.

INQUISITOR. Where is the mother?

CASTELLI. In Venice, I believe.

INQUISITOR. The mother in Venice. Galilei in Florence. What are his sex habits in Florence?

CASTELLI. I have no idea. I—

INQUISITOR. Is there a woman on the premises?

CASTELLI. No, there is no one—

INQUISITOR. Except you, eh? Does Galilei become too intimate with male companions? You are blushing: that is an answer in itself. Next question! Who is Monteverde? Another Hibernican? He is often mentioned in Galilei's conversation.

CASTELLI. He is a musician. Chorus master at St. Mark's.

INQUISITOR. St. Mark's, *Venice?* Once again, Venice?

CASTELLI. St. Mark's *is* in Venice.

INQUISITOR. Are you fencing with me? Don't pretend you don't know what the word *Venice* means today. Which brings us to our final question: when did Galilei launch his attack upon Holy Scripture?

CASTELLI. What attack upon Holy Scripture?!

INQUISITOR. So there were several? Mention whichever one comes to mind. *Pause.* Which one *has* come to mind?

CASTELLI. But he would *never* attack the Bible—

INQUISITOR. You say he "wouldn't." You are prevaricating. You were asked when *did* he. You are not a very cooperative witness, Father Castelli. This is serious: a priest who is not willing to fight heresy. But it is also *not* serious: it cannot seriously affect the history of the Holy Roman Inquisition. This investigation will continue.

D. A PHILANTHROPIST

Galileo's villa. Galileo is at his writing desk. Castelli is reading until there is a knock at an outside door and he leaves the room to attend to it. He returns.

CASTELLI. Galileo!

GALILEO, *deep in his writing.* Can't it wait?

CASTELLI. The grand duke's messenger! The grand duke is on his way over here!

GALILEO, *coming out of the cloud.* What?

CASTELLI. That's right. The grand duke is on his way. Here. Is about to make his entrance.

Cosimo II de' Medici became grand duke at the age of nineteen, and died at thirty-one. Jacques Callot, who was living in Florence during most of his reign, made this etching for his funeral ceremonies. The inscription reads: Master Scholar of the Order of Saint Stephen, Cosmus II Grand Duke of Tuscany. (Lieure, *Jacques Callot, Prints Division, New York Public Library. Aster, Lenox and Tilden Foundations*)

GALILEO. That doesn't happen! The grand duke of Tuscany doesn't enter the homes even of the richest merchants in town. . . .

CASTELLI. So what goes on?

GALILEO. Let's think. He returns from Leghorn. Hears all these rumors about me, the complaints, the suspicions, maybe even the accusations. Realizes my audience is coming up. His big announcement is coming up. Being a smart fellow, he also realizes that, if he just had ten minutes conversation with me, everything could be ironed out. So here he is. Huh? Is he?

CASTELLI. He will be, any moment. But I have another idea.

GALILEO. What?

CASTELLI. When he got back from the wars, a message from the Inquisition awaited him.

GALILEO. Your little inquisitor?

CASTELLI. Yes.

GALILEO. He is *too* little.

CASTELLI. The Inquisition is bigger.

GALILEO. I put my trust in Cosimo de' Medici!

A knock. Flunkeys enter and take up their stand on either side of the door. Grand Duke Cosimo enters with his chamberlain. The grand duke is a neat, "dynamic," self-assured young man, effusive without being warm, and bright without being intelligent, who today might become an executive in educational television. He might even be chosen to hand out funds for a philanthropic foundation. Like the Rockefellers, the Medici distributed largesse for cultural purposes. How the wealth had been acquired in the first place was and is a question not to be asked.

COSIMO. No, no! No formalities! This is a strictly informal visit. Incognito, one might say, except that everyone in Florence knows me. Well, so this is our celebrated mathematician! How do you like Florence? *One soon realizes that he never expects answers or comments.* It's a good city, isn't it, a handsome city! I want to thank you for your contribution to our culture. The city of Michelangelo—I say nothing of the Medici—appreciates culture. And since we've covered art and architecture, I think we should give science a whirl, don't you? Well, you're a biased witness on that one. I just wanted you to know our motives for bringing you here. You've got to cause future historians to write, "What Michelangelo was to painting and sculpture, Galileo was to science and philosophy." Let Bologna compete with that! And Venice too! Even Rome may get worried! You know how you got the job, I suppose? You don't? Well, that's important. There's a moral in it that I don't want you to miss. The man first in line for the job was a friend of yours—Father Sarpi? The combination of priest and scientist seemed pretty unbeatable. But it turns out he's a malcontent. Hostile to the Vatican, the Jesuits, all established authority. Regards the whole country as decadent, and so forth. Now there was criticism of you too, of course. You're a genius, after all. Temperamental. Make enemies wherever you go. But you don't hate established authority, do you? "Erratic, yes, but a lawabiding citizen and a good Catholic," said one of your testimonials. I said, "I'll buy that," and here you are. Now, Galilei, if you remember all this, everything is going to be all right. If you forget it, however, I won't be able to help you. Think it over and goodbye. My men will leave you some goodies to nibble on.

As they withdraw, Galileo plucks the chamberlain by the sleeve.

GALILEO. What happened, Niccolini?

CHAMBERLAIN. That agent of the Inquisition had an audience with Cosimo this morning.

He follows the others. When all have left, we realize they have left a pile of expensive food behind.

GALILEO. So?

CASTELLI. Galileo, I came to Florence in good faith, and ever since I've tried to make your wishes come true. But Sarpi and Sagredo were right.

GALILEO. We're in for a battle royal with the Dominicans and the Inquisition.

CASTELLI. The grand duke has proved a broken reed! We'll have to go back to Venice!

GALILEO. Venice?!

CASTELLI. What other escape route is there?

GALILEO. So Galileo's assistant talks the language of Sarpi. Escape route! *I am not a bad Catholic, Castelli.* I am not even against the Inquisition. If it is against *me,* I must face up to it, or at worst appeal to its leaders against its bureaucrats. Not back to Venice and the past! Forward to Rome!

CASTELLI. You hate Rome.

GALILEO. Rome, for good Catholics, is past, present, and future. I *need* Rome.

CASTELLI. What can you do there?

GALILEO. What did I do when my Paduan colleagues refused to look through the telescope?

CASTELLI. You went over their heads to the grand duke, and where has that got you?

GALILEO. Into hot water with the Dominicans and Inquisitors, so I'll go over *their* heads.

CASTELLI. Over the head of the Inquisition?

GALILEO. Over the head of its hirelings. For, if the hierarchy is not the church, your little preachers and investigators are not the hierarchy.

CASTELLI. Who *is* the hierarchy?

GALILEO. The man who condemned Bruno has "expressed a friendly interest" in the person and views of Galileo.

CASTELLI. Cardinal Bellarmine?

GALILEO. I shall go to Rome and appeal to Bellarmine in person. Are you coming with me?

Pause.

CASTELLI. Oh, I'll come with you.

GALILEO. We leave at dawn.

Portrait of Cardinal Bellarmine twelve years before his famous meeting with Galileo. In the background, left, the Antonine Column; right, Ignatius Loyola. On the table, a picture of Annunciation. Inscribed below: "Robertus Bellarminus Politianus, Cardinal of the Holy Roman Church, of Santa Maria in Via, Archbishop of Capua, most fierce defender of the Catholic Church against heretics, in his 62nd year. This is Bellarmine who crushed twin hydras: on the one hand by praise filled with his genius, on the other by his pious character. Franciscus Villamena made this engraving in Rome, 1604, with the privilege of the Supreme Pontiff and the authority of the high powers." (*Bibliothèque Nationale*)

Scene Four

THE MASTER OF CONTROVERSIAL QUESTIONS

Rome. Cardinal Bellarmine's audience chamber, which is empty save for Galileo and Castelli who sit waiting.

GALILEO. How many days is it he has kept us waiting?

CASTELLI. Fifty-five.

GALILEO. Nearly two months. Maybe I made a mistake presenting my case in writing. I should have got an appointment two months ago and refused to leave till every point was driven home.

CASTELLI. The delay *could* mean he's taking you seriously. Your project is hardly one that a cardinal could take in stride.

GALILEO. My project?

CASTELLI. Asking the Catholic Church to change its mind.

A secretary enters.

SECRETARY. The Lord Cardinal Bellarmine.

The man who now enters in the red robes of his office is a wizened little creature with keen, mischievous eyes. He has the poise of one who both enjoys the exercise of power and is accustomed to it. He is so far from feeling the need for an aggressive style that he invites characterization as a frail old man and cups an ear in his hand from time to time to suggest deafness. Certainly one feels that he does not hear certain things; whether he is deaf or not is another question. He is not senile.

BELLARMINE. Professor Galilei?

GALILEO, *kissing his ring.* And this is Father Castelli, my assistant. *Castelli kisses the cardinal's ring too.*

BELLARMINE, *placing himself presidentially behind a table, smiling.* Well! A historic occasion. The meeting of Bellarmine and Galileo

43

An artist's image, not reliably identified, of one of Galileo's confrontations, presumably that with Bellarmine dramatized in the present scene. Nineteenth century? (*Bettmann Archive*)

could hardly *fail* to be a historic occasion. Forgive me if I do not underestimate my own importance. Do you know what the king of England calls me? The Red Menace! Also the Devil's best friend. So I *am* important. Ironically speaking. You are important *un*ironically speaking. . . . So the best friend of the Devil is meeting the best friend of Science!

GALILEO. I'm flattered that you've interested yourself in my little exploits, Your Eminence.

BELLARMINE. My God, you have all the mock humility of a bishop! Little exploits! Young Barberini knows all about science and can't stop talking about you. Quotes you by the yard—delights to go "wandering and discoursing with you among truths"!

GALILEO. You have been reading *me,* Your Eminence!

BELLARMINE. Did I quote you correctly?

GALILEO. "How great a sweetness to go wandering and discoursing together among truths!"

BELLARMINE. "How great a joy to proceed from true principles to true conclusions!" Correct?

GALILEO. Correct.

They chuckle.

BELLARMINE. But of course you're anxious to get down to business?

GALILEO. I won't say no to that, Your Eminence.

BELLARMINE, *to the secretary.* Ask Father Scheiner to come in, would you? *To Galileo.* You know Scheiner, of course.

GALILEO. We met in Padua. Since which time he has become the leading Jesuit scientist.

BELLARMINE. Quarreled with you lately, didn't he?

GALILEO. He claimed to have discovered the sun spots before I did. That was . . . inexact.

CASTELLI. That was false.

GALILEO. Oh, come, Castelli, Scheiner is an ally. Through him, Jesuit science has committed itself to Copernicus. And what the Jesuits say today, the church will say tomorrow, eh, Your Eminence?

BELLARMINE, *who has been consulting documents.* Eh, what? Oh, yes, we Jesuits have a certain standing these days. The church cannot easily ignore us. No, indeed.

While he is saying this, Father Scheiner is shown in. The two scientists eye each other. Bellarmine talks right on. He consults documents from time to time throughout his presentation.

Another historic encounter! Our greatest scientific priest meets our greatest scientific layman! Well, be seated, gentlemen, and let's proceed at once. I must first enjoin secrecy upon you pending our public announcement. Father Scheiner, you will keep the minutes for the Inquisition records. That way we will be sure they are scientifically correct.

CASTELLI. May I keep notes for Professor Galilei?

BELLARMINE. Good idea, good idea. Now, let me begin by putting you out of your agony, Galilei. The goings-on have been scandalous. They will stop. Forthwith and forever. All harassment will cease. No sermon will be preached against you ever again. No gossip will be spread against you by monks and priests. As for the blunders of the Inquisition itself, or rather of some of its officious menials, they will not recur. Father Castelli, our apologies if some of the Lord's watchdogs have proved to be donkeys.

GALILEO. You see, Castelli, what did I tell you?

BELLARMINE. Not only, Professor, does your church apologize for the clumsiness of its servants, and free you from all suspicions spread by them, we come to you in gratitude for the service you now render us. While our people squander their energies in slander and intrigue against you, you recall us to our proper duties. For seventy-three years this book of Copernicus has lain around. A few of us read it. None of us came to grips with it. You have forced us to study it, reflect upon it, and commit the church to a definite view of it. *He pauses grandly.*

GALILEO, *on tenterhooks.* Yes? Yes, Your Eminence?

BELLARMINE, *searching among his papers.* I was looking for our official formulation. Of the main point, you know: The universe? Earth-round-sun or sun-round-earth? Ah yes. *He coughs, then reads.* "The following opinions, having been submitted for analysis to the experts of the Inquisition, namely, that the sun does not move round the earth and that the earth does move round the sun, both opinions have been declared false, absurd, and contrary to the Bible."

GALILEO. What?

SCHEINER. But our observations confirm Professor Galilei's, Your Eminence! We now know that the sun does *not* move round the earth and that the earth *does* move round the sun!

BELLARMINE, *still immersed in his document.* Father Scheiner, we shall get to you in a minute. *Coughs again and reads.* "The Lord Cardinal Bellarmine is therefore instructed to summon Galilei before him and advise him not in future to defend these opinions."

GALILEO. They have turned me down flat? I can't believe it.

BELLARMINE, *continuing.* "As for researches of a Copernican nature within the confines of the church herself, they will cease. Laboratories and observatories will close down. Our physicists all being Jesuits, they will scarcely need reminding of their vows. The Vicar-General is hereby instructed to enforce that absolute obedience for which the Society is so justly renowned."

SCHEINER. But this is impossible, Your Eminence! The earth does move round the sun! Who has advised you to the contrary? On what grounds? Why didn't you respect our own Jesuit observatories?

BELLARMINE. It's a shock, yes. You'll need time to adjust, I realize that. All this work for nothing! Very galling for you both, I realize that too. But we shall make it up to you. You're ambitious men. We shall not frustrate your ambitions. For luckily, you are versatile. Your ambitions will take a different direction when they must. *Turning to Galileo.* The man who could invent the pendulum, the thermometer, and the telescope can invent something else. Why don't you invent me a gun, Galilei? Some firearm that the Protestants don't have. Then the right side will always win, hm? Invent me a gun. As for you, Father Scheiner, the Inquisition needs a man who knows more of heresy than the heretics themselves. You are that man. You shall be our Special Adviser on Scientific Affairs and as such have far more power than you ever had as a mere researcher.

SCHEINER, *his eyes starting out of his head.* This is a nightmare! How can I sit in judgment on people I agree with? And "agreement" isn't the word. These are not opinions, they are objective facts. How can I renounce facts for fantasies? Perhaps I *am* a man who enjoys power. But as a priest I seek purity. As a scientist I revere truth. How then shall I—

BELLARMINE. Father Scheiner, you are overexcited, which is excusable in the circumstances. Leave us. You need time, solitude. You also have a job to do: enter this day's business in the minutes. Here's the original I was reading from. *Gives him a couple of sheets of paper but Scheiner seems rooted to the spot.* Leave us.

SCHEINER, *in a low voice.* Has it not occurred to you what this experience will do *to me?*

BELLARMINE. What? What are you talking about?

SCHEINER. An ambitious Jesuit. No saint. An intellectual. And now a frustrated intellectual. An intellectual whose arm has been twisted. Whose soul will have been twisted. Don't make a dangerous man of me, Your Eminence!

BELLARMINE. By no means. Of every Jesuit we make an obedient man. Obedient men are the reverse of dangerous. Obey me now by leaving—without another word. *Scheiner is starting to speak.* Without another word. *Scheiner leaves. Pause. Galileo also starts to leave.*

BELLARMINE. I trust you understand, Professor, why this must be?

GALILEO. What is that?

BELLARMINE. You know how things are, in the Christendom of today?

GALILEO. How are they?

BELLARMINE. You are unworldly in a new sense, Galilei. Your thoughts are in those other worlds of yours and not in this one!

GALILEO. Does this one insist on being stationary?

BELLARMINE. Ask rather if it insists on becoming Protestant. When one country falls to this new enemy, must they all go—like dominoes?* At least we can say this much, not one more will go. Further encroachment will be stopped on all fronts! *Smiling at his own fervor.*

---

* Dominoes do not seem to have been traced back earlier in Europe than the eighteenth century. But this is hardly the first time that a history play contained anachronisms. In any case, what characters say should seem to be what such persons (give or take elements of style imposed by the context) would indeed say. Seem—to whom? To the audience. And our audiences have no clue to the answer except their own experience of such people. It was the opinion of the present author that his audience had often heard their Bellarmines talk about dominoes. (Actually, dominoes here are not "out of time" but "out of place," since they did exist in China.)

Well, Professor, I am Master of Controversial Questions. Commander in Chief on the intellectual front, so to speak.

GALILEO, *unsmiling*. Copernicus was no Protestant. His teaching was dismissed as folly by both Luther and Calvin.

BELLARMINE. And they were *really* the Devil's best friends, I agree, allies of Satan, enemies of God! For a hundred years now, Protestantism has drawn to itself all elements of doubt and dissent, so that, by this time, all elements of doubt and dissent lend comfort to Protestantism. In combating this evil thing, Galilei, we combat the incarnate spirit of innovation.

GALILEO. But I can't see you rejecting a doctrine, not because it's false, but because it's new!

BELLARMINE, *mildly*. My dear Professor, the new is bound to be false. We Catholics say to the Protestants, "Since you are changeable, you cannot be the truth."

GALILEO. We Copernicans say to scientists who will not learn, "Since you are unchangeable, you must be dead."

BELLARMINE, *cupping his ear in his hand*. What? What was that?

GALILEO. I was taught: "We limit not the truth of God."

BELLARMINE, *still seeming not to hear*. What? What's this?

GALILEO. "The Lord hath yet more light and truth to break forth from his word."

BELLARMINE. Oh. By whom? By whom were you taught that?

GALILEO. By my dear departed mother.

BELLARMINE. Hm. Were she alive, we should have to have that looked into. Must I instruct you in the Catholic faith, Galilei? The truth, as you well know, has been revealed once and for all. It has also been brought down to us by a mother who has not departed. Mother Church. *Again relaxing, with a smile.* What would you think, after all, of a God who withheld the truth from countless generations and then suddenly popped it exclusively into the brains of Canon Copernicus and Professor Galilei?

GALILEO, *again not returning the smile*. What do *you* think of the curiosity which God implanted in Copernicus and Galilei—through which they must inevitably discover things and formulate new truths?

BELLARMINE. Hm. Curiosity is as curiosity does. And in our time it does ill. Haven't you noticed, Galilei, that, today, "daring" thoughts are the Devil's favorite bait? What is your field? Yes, mathematics —a subject that has its fascination, that's the trouble! We know, from the Bible, that, at Doomsday, the stars will fall from the sky. All right, find me one modern mathematician who doesn't want to contest this! Some of them have even proved that stars cannot fall! *The smile vanishes.* Men, my dear Galilei, are like frogs: openmouthed to the lure of things that don't concern them. The Devil, being a good fisherman, catches them in shoals. *Sadly.* So when I hear the word curiosity, I summon my Inquisitors, and we prepare the faggots for the stake.

Pause.

GALILEO. Suppose I say, "the earth does move round the sun." What do you reply?

BELLARMINE. That it does not. What could be simpler?

GALILEO. I provided physical evidence. Did you understand it?

BELLARMINE. No.

GALILEO. Well then.

BELLARMINE. Well then what? Evidence must be understandable, or it is not evidence.

GALILEO. I will not ask, understandable by whom? But if I were to come back to you at some future date with outright proof would you then be willing to say that the earth moves round the sun?

BELLARMINE. Of course!

GALILEO. Of course?

BELLARMINE. I am a logician, and you have asked me a question to which the logical answer is Yes. But you placed an *if* before the question. I do not regard the condition it implies as fulfillable— except insofar as all things are possible to Him above. *He crosses himself.*

GALILEO. But since all things are possible to Him above, this too is possible to Him above.

BELLARMINE. Persuasion would be needed as well as proof. And up to now you have shown little interest in persuading us. Mother Church, my dear Professor, cannot be raped!

GALILEO. Can she be seduced?

BELLARMINE. By proof and persuasion.

GALILEO. But I'm not allowed to offer proof and persuasion.

BELLARMINE. How's that?

GALILEO. To quote your decree, now being entered in the Inquisition minutes by Father Scheiner.

BELLARMINE. To misquote it. Read him the text, Castelli.

CASTELLI, *consulting his notes.* ". . . Summon . . . Galileo . . . and advise him not in future to defend these opinions."

GALILEO. Exactly.

BELLARMINE. They wouldn't be *opinions* if you proved them to be facts. Nor do facts need a defense. Merely a persuasive presentation.

GALILEO. You are suggesting, then—

BELLARMINE. Mother Church is never indifferent to truth or deaf to persuasion. Remember that.

GALILEO. I shall. *And he again starts to leave.* And yet you say, Your Eminence, that the sun moves round the earth. Is it impertinent to ask how you know that?

BELLARMINE. Not at all. It is clearly implied in the Bible. Joshua commanded the sun to stand still. You will agree that this would make no sense if the sun was *already* standing still. As a Christian you will also agree that the word of God always makes sense.

GALILEO. Cardinal Barberini has been quoted to a somewhat different effect.

BELLARMINE. Oh?

GALILEO. "The aim of the Bible is to teach us how to go to Heaven, not to teach us how the Heavens go."

BELLARMINE. Ts, ts, ts. The Bible cannot be wrong. Did Our Lord believe that the earth moved round the sun?

GALILEO. One would hardly suppose so.

BELLARMINE. Yet He was perfect. And said in so many words, "I am the Way, the *Truth,* and the Life." Or, as the Apostle puts it, "Jesus Christ the same yesterday and today and forever." You are not perfect, Galileo. If we have refrained from pointing out your imperfections, it is because we do not wish to discourage you. We admire you. All men are sinners, however, and the Devil has world-shaking designs on men of world-shaking talent. It is possible that he has already injected the Protestant virus into your bloodstream. If so, you will need all your resources to combat it. And God's help. You will be with me in my prayers tonight, Galileo. May I be in yours?

And Bellarmine leaves, followed by the secretary. Galileo and Castelli do not move.

GALILEO. So we go back to Florence, I invent "something useful," the Inquisition leaves me alone, the priests praise me from their pulpits, and my sainted mother can look down from Heaven and be proud of me. Why do they speak of something useful when all they mean is something that kills more Germans? And why am I a great man when I make a new killing machine but not when I help people to see the glory of His handiwork?

CASTELLI. You won't be able to live with this.

GALILEO. If the earth does not go round the sun, that is not just a little miscalculation in Professor Galilei's exercise book, it is something radically wrong both with Galilei himself and with the science to which he has devoted his life. "Not an opinion but a fact"—Scheiner's words. He will have to eat them. But I am not a Jesuit. I don't have to eat them. *Pause.* What *do* I have to do?

CASTELLI. Get away from here at all costs!

GALILEO. Huh?

CASTELLI. Leave Rome, leave Florence. It would be safest to leave Italy.

GALILEO. Well, at least you haven't told me to return to the Venetian Republic.

CASTELLI. Can you face exile?

GALILEO. I am not interested in exile. Am I a Protestant?

CASTELLI. Of course not.

GALILEO. Bellarmine has a point. If I left Catholic soil, I *would* be giving the Protestants aid and comfort.

CASTELLI. Then there's nothing for it but knuckling under. *Trying to smile.* Perhaps it won't be so bad. Your next book wasn't to be about the universe anyway, was it?

GALILEO. It's to be about motion. Mechanics.

CASTELLI. What are you thinking, maestro?

GALILEO. The book on motion will have to wait.

CASTELLI. How's that?

GALILEO. Do I really have to choose between exile and silence? Between outright mutiny and utter servility?

CASTELLI. Yes. Yes!

GALILEO. You are forgetting Bellarmine's lesson in logic. *If* I can be persuasive, *if* I can present what are conceded to be proofs, I can still "defend Copernicus," can still study cosmology.

CASTELLI. "Persuasiveness" is not a scientific category. Bellarmine can find you unpersuasive to all eternity.

GALILEO. Bellarmine won't live to all eternity. I will write a new book— on this subject, not some other. Bellarmine won't be around by the time it's finished. Think of the new generation. They say Barberini will be the next pope. He'll free us from this bondage. Me *and* Father Scheiner. Think of Scheiner's delight—to be allowed to return to his old haunts!

CASTELLI. Will he be delighted to learn that science owes all this to you and nothing to him?

GALILEO. Father Castelli, you should be ashamed of yourself. I have more belief in churchmen and the church than *you* have. The church is bound to be right in the end; for that reason I have faith that it is going to support me in the beginning. Will you play the unbeliever, priest?

CASTELLI. I fear Scheiner.

GALILEO. What can he do?

CASTELLI. Well, suppose what he writes into the minutes is inaccurate?

GALILEO. He would hardly falsify Inquisition records.

CASTELLI. He lied about the sunspots.

GALILEO. Under pressure of acute professional rivalry.

CASTELLI. Exactly.

Pause.

GALILEO. Did you get down what Bellarmine said?

CASTELLI. Yes.

GALILEO. Go back to him. Ask him to certify that your transcript is correct.

CASTELLI. I'll catch him before he leaves the building.

Starts to leave.

GALILEO. Oh, and Castelli, when you have his signature, just casually throw out that I'm on the track of a new explosive. Far more damaging than anything on the market so far.

CASTELLI. But is that true?

GALILEO. No. Yes. Only don't tell him this part: it is for use "on the intellectual front." For blowing up the world—all the worlds—in which Bellarmine believes.

CASTELLI. You mean the book.

GALILEO. Yes. Are you going to stay with me to work on it?

CASTELLI. How long will it take?

GALILEO, *after a moment's thought.* Oh, give me fifteen years.

Castelli leaves.

Title page of *Two World Systems* as published by the Elzevirs of Leyden, Holland, in 1635. The three figures are Aristotle, Ptolemy, and Copernicus. (*Bettmann Archive*)

Scene Five

TWO WORLD SYSTEMS

The same Florentine villa as in Scene Three. But many years have passed since the previous scenes.* It is almost sunset on a bright March afternoon. The table is already laid for supper. Sound of a coach halting outside. A knock on the house door. Castelli emerges from an unseen room and crosses to the door. He is now in his thirties. He opens the door. Virginia—Sister Maria—enters. She is no longer a girl.

CASTELLI. Sister Maria! At last! Why, it's so good to see you!
He embraces her.

VIRGINIA. Your message was so mysterious. "Come at once. Explanations on arrival." The mother superior almost didn't let me come.

CASTELLI. She never lets you come these days. How many months since the last time?

* Why not say *how* many? History has not concealed the answer. It is seventeen. But to the extent that our scenes are viewed as drama, rather than pure chronicle, they are also viewed as performance and in the theatre the passage of time can easily become obtrusive. Seeing Helen Hayes present Queen Victoria, her audiences used to ask, how old will she be in the next scene? and often asked nothing else. In the present script, the number of years is left unstated so that the actors need not focus their attention, and the public's, on time and its effects upon the human body, the greying hair, the stooping shoulders, the quavering voice. This was the more important because the time span from the death of Giordano Bruno to the trial of Galileo was all of thirty-three years. The literal-minded stage director would face many problems. Not only would his Galileo have to age inordinately. Two actresses would be needed for the one role of his daughter (little girl and woman). Yet these are problems which not only can but should be avoided. Though passage of time is important in this action as a painful process of waiting and also as developing conflict, the biological ageing process has no part in it whatever. This Galileo is not shown in the blindness of his later years. He is never even shown as an old man. The thirty-three years of history may properly seem about twenty. If an audience never even asks itself how many years have passed, that is perhaps the most desirable result of all.

VIRGINIA. Six. It was before the death of the holy father. We went into strict seclusion after that.

Castelli has taken her cloak and shawl and brought her into the living room.

CASTELLI. I'm afraid the holy father's death didn't sadden *your* father. *She winces.* I shouldn't have put it that way.

VIRGINIA. *I* shouldn't be so touchy. You see, at the convent, I'm the one whose father quarreled with the pope.

She knows her father's home and finds her own way to a seat. In his personal life, Galileo belongs to these two, Virginia and Castelli, and they especially feel their common proprietorship when they meet after long absence and when they are alone together. Both conditions are met now.

CASTELLI. Well, he won't, now. When Barberini was elected pope your father staged a celebration. All Florence was here. The archbishop of Florence read a message from Barberini to the assembled company. From Pope Urban, I should say.

VIRGINIA. Where *is* my father?

CASTELLI. Out gardening. He got tired of sitting here waiting for the mailcoach.

VIRGINIA. Mailcoach?

CASTELLI. That belongs to the "explanations on arrival."

VIRGINIA. Oh? I thought they'd have something to do with The Book.

CASTELLI. They do.

VIRGINIA. Don't say it's finished? After how many years is it?

CASTELLI. It was as if he couldn't bear to finish it while the old pope was still around. Less than three weeks after Barberini's accession, he marched in here one morning, and plonked the completed manuscript down on that table.

A small, high table occupies pretty much the proud place in this room as the reading stand had in the Padua house in Scene One.

VIRGINIA. You don't mean *that's* it? *She jumps up to touch some pages of the manuscript.* Hm. Is this the only copy?

During this speech, her father has entered by a door that leads directly to the garden. He is dressed in old gardening clothes, has a couple of gardening tools dangling from his waist, and some foliage in one hand. Since we last saw him he has passed from early to late middle age. He is a little frailer in body but, if anything, even more purposeful and vigorous in mind.

GALILEO. "Explanations on arrival"!

VIRGINIA, *turning round.* Father! *And she runs to embrace him.*

GALILEO. Well, my dear, you're so pretty these days, a father could have unmonastic thoughts.

VIRGINIA. And you're still the Greek god: ageless. Your eyes are about nineteen.

Castelli realizes that father and daughter would like to be alone for a while.

CASTELLI. I'll go see if the mailcoach has come. *He leaves by the house door.*

GALILEO. Will you drink a little wine with me before supper? I sent to the ends of the earth for it.

VIRGINIA. Sicily, you mean. I'd love some. But why don't you put those leaves down first?

GALILEO. They're for the wine. Watch. I take this leaf, fold it like this, make little holes in it with a pin like this, dip the stalk in the wine like this, take the leaf in my mouth like this, and suck up the wine through the little holes like this.

VIRGINIA. What for?

GALILEO. To get more pleasure from the wine. Watch again!

He continues with his experiment.

VIRGINIA. "The body, like the mind, should imbibe delicately."

GALILEO, *between imbibings.* What?

VIRGINIA. You made me write that out three times—when I was ten.

GALILEO. Heavens, was I that stuffy? Well, today I thought of a definition of wine.

VIRGINIA. Oh?

GALILEO. "Wine . . . is light held together by moisture."

VIRGINIA. That's beautiful!

GALILEO. It would even be clear—but for one thing.

VIRGINIA. What's that?

GALILEO. I don't know what light is. Want to try this? *He offers her a leaf.*

Portrait of Benedetto Castelli (*Alinari*)

VIRGINIA, *who has already been drinking from a glass.* I'm very content with this.

Silence. They sit drinking, each in his own way.

Castelli told me about the book. It must give you a deep feeling of satisfaction to have finished it at last.

GALILEO. I'm on top of the world. Never been so happy in all my life. *Another sip.* People sneer at success. I wonder if they should: it seems to do one good. I'm savoring it—as I do this wine—and finding a lot more nourishment in it.

VIRGINIA. And now what?

GALILEO. Castelli hadn't finished his story? Where'd he leave off?

VIRGINIA. I was asking if that, *pointing to the manuscript,* was the only copy.

GALILEO, *jumping straight in.* It's one of two copies.

VIRGINIA. Where's the other?

GALILEO, *with relish.* The other? The other is on Pope Urban's desk in the Vatican.

VIRGINIA. Good heavens, is it that kind of book?

GALILEO. How d'you mean?

VIRGINIA. Well, d'you need the Holy Father's special . . . patronage?

GALILEO. You don't know what it's about, do you?

VIRGINIA. You have never breathed a word in all the years.

GALILEO. Because I'm going to present you with a *fait accompli:* a book on a "highly controversial subject" licensed by the Holy Father.

VIRGINIA. So *that's* why you're on top of the world. When did the news come?

GALILEO. It should have come several hours ago. We tried to time your arrival for right afterwards. But the mailcoach is late.

VIRGINIA. So that's what Castelli's doing out there—

GALILEO. Getting the pope's letter from the mailman—

VIRGINIA. The letter authorizing publication of your book!

GALILEO. Such was the "explanation on arrival."

VIRGINIA. So it's quite certain? Pope Urban has let you know he *will* approve?

GALILEO. Oh, he committed himself to our views years ago.

VIRGINIA. But now he's pope.

GALILEO. Pah! Barberini is a man of character.

VIRGINIA. And couldn't have reasons for changing?

GALILEO. You can't withdraw support from a case that has been proved.

Castelli comes hurrying in, holding up an envelope.

CASTELLI. The papal coat of arms on the envelope!

Galileo snatches the letter, opens it with trembling fingers, quickly skims the contents in silence, then grunts non-committally.

VIRGINIA, *also on her feet by now.* Has he *not* approved the book?

GALILEO. Sit down, both of you. Now, Castelli, read this letter for the three of us.

Castelli, having taken the letter back, reads, sitting.

CASTELLI. "Dear Professor Galilei, the Holy Father has received your request for a license to publish your manuscript *The Two World Systems.* . . ."

VIRGINIA. *Two World Systems!* So that's what the book is!

CASTELLI. ". . . Kindly present yourself without delay at the address below. Signed, Firenzuola, Commissar General." The address below is the Palace of Inquisition in Rome.

VIRGINIA. The Inquisition!

GALILEO. So how do my two henchmen take this new turn in the story?

VIRGINIA. That subject has always made trouble between you and the church.

GALILEO. "The hierarchy is not the church."

CASTELLI. You're prepared to take on the hierarchy now?

GALILEO. What should I do? Present myself without delay at the address below?

VIRGINIA. You have to. When the Inquisition sends for you.

GALILEO. Castelli?

CASTELLI. This is a very great setback.

GALILEO. And?

CASTELLI. In going to Rome you are putting your head in the she-wolf's mouth.

GALILEO. But as Virginia says, I have no alternative. Save flight, save exile. And I would rather all my books were burned, I would rather tear out my right eye, than lend comfort in any way to the enemies of our church.

CASTELLI. In Rome you confront the top men of the hierarchy.

GALILEO. They have my confidence!

CASTELLI. But this letter!

GALILEO. The pope is busy. He had the right to hand the book on to—

CASTELLI. He can understand the book. The commissar of the Inquisition can *not*.

GALILEO. The commissar has the cardinals of the Holy Office to advise him—

CASTELLI. The cardinals! But the cardinals are—

VIRGINIA. You're wasting your breath, Castelli. Look at his face. He is going to Rome.

GALILEO, *to Castelli.* And once again you are coming with me.

CASTELLI, *sighing.* I suppose I am.

GALILEO. Enough gravity then. *To Virginia.* You are our guest at supper tonight. Drink a toast with me. *He has poured the wine. They take their glasses.* I give you the friendship of both your fathers, Virginia, the holy one in Rome and the somewhat less holy one here in Florence!

They touch glasses.

An artist's image of Galileo before the Inquisition. Probably nineteenth century. (*Bettmann Archive*)

Scene Six

THE INQUISITION

Rome. In the Palace of the Inquisition. Again, as before Bellarmine years earlier, Galileo sits with the faithful Castelli awaiting word from above.

GALILEO. So here we are: in the Palace of the Inquisition. Is it so terrifying?
If he means the surroundings, they are indeed unterrifying: they are elegant.
CASTELLI. The room is set up for a formal proceeding.
Tables and chairs are arranged for a council or other such proceeding.
GALILEO. But when the secretary said, the Commissar General will be here in a moment, I got the impression he'd come alone. What do you know about him?
CASTELLI. He's one of the new men. Name of Firenzuola. Very close to the Vatican. Not so close to the Jesuits.
GALILEO. In other words, it's *preferable* to deal with him alone.
CASTELLI. Definitely.
A secretary enters.
SECRETARY. Father Commissar Firenzuola.
The Commissar General of the Inquisition enters. Father Firenzuola is a pleasant-looking young official, and in his handling of the business in hand will prove brisk, efficient, and correct. All associations with the word "Inquisition" would only mislead us as to his character, since he is not a villain either of the blustering or the smooth variety. He sees himself—and after all is not alone in this—simply as a man with a job to do for an organization that has made certain commitments. He is not an ideologue, and feels no animus against Galileo.

FIRENZUOLA. Would you sit here, Professor?

They have never met, but Firenzuola takes in Galileo at a glance, Castelli at a second glance. The secretary has already left.

And perhaps we should be alone for a few minutes.

GALILEO. I would prefer it if Castelli could remain.

CASTELLI. The professor isn't as young as he once was, Father Commissar.

GALILEO. I'm not as bright as I once was. I need Castelli to prompt me, these days.

FIRENZUOLA. As a priest Father Castelli knows the meaning of secrecy. He shall stay if you say so.

GALILEO. Thank you.

FIRENZUOLA. Galilei, you have submitted a manuscript for a publication license. I have to report that your petition has been denied.

GALILEO, *turning to Castelli, unable to believe his ears.* What? The request . . . denied?

FIRENZUOLA, *who does not leave such questions for others to handle.* The book cannot possibly be approved. We are amazed that you should ever have supposed it could be. But since you did, we recognize that this news must come to you as a shock. And we know a good deal about shocks. One needs time to get over them. Would you care to return to this room in exactly forty-eight hours?

GALILEO, *and it is not clear now if he is speaking to Castelli, to Firenzuola, or himself.* The book "cannot possibly be approved"?

FIRENZUOLA. That is correct.

GALILEO. Not even in amended form?

FIRENZUOLA. Not even in amended form.

GALILEO. Selections from it could appear perhaps?

FIRENZUOLA. No, no, Professor. There are no if's or but's. The answer is an all-inclusive no.

GALILEO. I can't take this in.

FIRENZUOLA. That is why we suggest a two-day recess.

GALILEO, *suddenly much clearer in his mind.* Oh, no, no, no. Time won't help. I'll stay.

FIRENZUOLA. Are you sure?

GALILEO. I'll stay.

FIRENZUOLA. You are a strong man, and we admire strength. To proceed. As you must know better than anyone, Professor, in this book you have championed a view of the universe which the church condemned years ago. We will not discuss that view; or the church's condemnation of it; nor yet your . . . defiance of the condemnation. We will content ourselves with a repetition of our first statement. *Your book is banned.* It has been condemned by the congregation of the Holy Office, and this condemnation will be enforced by the Inquisition. Need I say more? You know why the Inquisition exists. You know how it operates. You know you mustn't oppose its wishes. You know you would get nowhere if you did. . . . You follow me?

GALILEO. Hm? Oh. Oh, yes, I am following you very intently, Father Commissar.

FIRENZUOLA. Good. Because I am going to propose something. Doing it will hurt, but believe me when I say that not doing it would hurt far, far more. And we know a good deal about hurts, too. *He stops as if for a reaction.*

GALILEO. Yes, yes?

FIRENZUOLA. Allow us to destroy your manuscript. Destroy any other copies you may have made. Drop the whole matter. And the world will never know you have been condemned by us, nor even that we ever received a manuscript. No punishment, no disgrace, no censure, no slur on your good name. You will walk out of here a free man.

GALILEO. I see. *Slowly.* Free to do what?

FIRENZUOLA. *You* tell *us.* To pursue your researches in mathematics and physics . . . in any direction whatever, any *other* direction whatever . . . perhaps something more practical . . . ?

GALILEO. Ah yes, I should invent a gun.

FIRENZUOLA. What was that?

GALILEO. Oh, just something Bellarmine told me.

FIRENZUOLA, *not to be sidetracked.* So you do accept our proposal?

GALILEO. Of burning my book?

FIRENZUOLA. Of . . . wiping the slate clean?

GALILEO. No, no, I can't.

FIRENZUOLA. Galilei, we are *prepared* for a negative answer, and our preparations are cruel. Humiliating. Are you determined to make us use them?

GALILEO. I cannot burn my book.

FIRENZUOLA. If you and I fail to reach agreement, the entire matter will be placed in the hands of six cardinals of the Holy Office. At once. They are waiting in the next room now. None of them has read your book. They will be dependent on a single reader: your old rival Father Scheiner, the Special Adviser on Scientific Affairs.

GALILEO. I am sure Father Scheiner can do a good job.

FIRENZUOLA, *hesitating.* He is a Jesuit. *Pause.* So are three of the cardinals.

GALILEO, *smoothly.* I am not prejudiced against the Society of Jesus, Father Commissar.

FIRENZUOLA. You know best. *He rings a bell. A secretary enters.* Ask the cardinals to come in now, would you? *The secretary at once admits six cardinals who take seats obviously prepared for them and soon look like a bench of judges. What manner of men are they? Are they religious? Are they ecclesiastical, even? It is debatable. What is certain is that these are men in important positions in an organization that dominates the life of the time. They resemble other such men.*

FIRENZUOLA. Would you now care to reconsider my proposal, Professor? *Galileo shakes his head.*

FIRENZUOLA, *to the secretary.* Ask Father Scheiner to come in. *To Galileo.* You may find him somewhat changed.

Father Scheiner comes in. He is recognizable but terribly changed. He was gaunt before but is now gaunter. His eyes were fiery before but are now deepset, haunted. His face is unnaturally pale. He too takes a place obviously prepared for him. When all are in position, Firenzuola continues. My lords, the question before you this morning is whether to license the book *The Two World Systems* by Galileo Galilei, who has generously consented to be present with us. You will be assisted in making this decision by the Special Adviser on Scientific Affairs and myself. Your decision will be reached unanimously, as per the regulations. Yes, Cardinal Silotti? *Cardinal 1 has held up his hand.*

CARDINAL 1. May not a decision also be reached by five votes to one?

FIRENZUOLA. That is correct. *Reading from a small book on his desk.* "Provided an honest and exhaustive attempt at unanimity has been made and on no account on the first day of such proceeding."

CARDINAL 1. Thank you.

FIRENZUOLA. The Special Adviser has studied the book and researched the entire career of its author. Father Scheiner?

SCHEINER. Yes, Father Commissar?

FIRENZUOLA. Question Galilei on his meeting with Cardinal Bellarmine.

SCHEINER, *stepping forward.* Galilei, it is my understanding that you met with Cardinal Bellarmine, on a single occasion, more than ten years ago, is that so?

GALILEO. That is so.

SCHEINER. Could you tell the tribunal what the upshot of the meeting was?

GALILEO. I was advised not to defend the forbidden doctrine of Copernicus.

SCHEINER. Not to . . . . What was the verb?

GALILEO. Defend.

SCHEINER. Galilei, I have here in my hand the words of Bellarmine as set down in the Inquisition records at the time. Would you be exact in your account?

GALILEO. I have been exactly exact, that is my profession.

SCHEINER. Then, Father Commissar, may I read the actual words of Bellarmine?

FIRENZUOLA. Please do.

SCHEINER. "Galilei was enjoined to relinquish the opinion that the sun is the center of the world and stationary and that the earth is not the center of the world and is not stationary and forbidden to discuss *or even mention it in any way,* orally or in writing, which injunction the said Galilei agreed to and promised to obey."

GALILEO. *Discuss or even mention in any way?!* But Bellarmine even went on to say that I could offer proofs and persuasions—which is exactly what my new manuscript does!

FIRENZUOLA. Is there anything to that effect in the minutes?

SCHEINER. No, Father Commissar.

FIRENZUOLA. Are the Inquisition minutes generally accurate and complete in such matters?

SCHEINER. They are the most accurate and complete records in the world.

FIRENZUOLA, *to Galileo.* Now you know what I mean by cruel and humiliating. You have forced us to convict you of breach of faith with your church.

GALILEO. But I deny it! A man couldn't forget being ordered not to mention his favorite subject, the theme of his whole life's work!

FIRENZUOLA. Precisely.

GALILEO. I know I never agreed to that.

CASTELLI. May we see those minutes, Father Commissar?

SCHEINER. That would be extremely irregular, Father Commissar.

FIRENZUOLA. Let him see them.

They are handed to Castelli.

CASTELLI. It is as I feared. The handwriting is different. The minute was not written by the same hand as everything else in this section of the book.

SCHEINER. May I speak to that?

FIRENZUOLA. You may.

SCHEINER. The minute in question was written by me. Castelli already knew that. He heard Bellarmine order that.

FIRENZUOLA. Father Castelli, scientific notes written up by Father Scheiner could only be considered more than usually dependable.

CASTELLI. He had always been jealous of Galileo. And it was a moment of very great stress for him.

Pause.

FIRENZUOLA. You couldn't be suggesting that Father Scheiner falsified our records?

GALILEO. It *is* a falsification, so, if Scheiner wrote it. . . .

FIRENZUOLA. In any event, wild accusations made on the spur of the moment by way of effective speechmaking cannot weigh in the balance against official records.

GALILEO. What would you accept as legitimate evidence on our side?

FIRENZUOLA. We would need Bellarmine's signature on a written document.

GALILEO. We have that.

CASTELLI, *rooting among his papers.* Indeed, yes. I noticed at the time the state Father Scheiner was in. Here. *He hands it to Firenzuola.*

FIRENZUOLA. "The following opinions . . . that the sun does not move round the earth and that the earth does move around the sun . . . have been declared false. . . . Cardinal Bellarmine is therefore instructed to summon Galilei before him and advise him not in future to defend these opinions. Signed, Robert Cardinal Bellarmine."

Silence.

SCHEINER. May I see that document, Father Commissar? It will be a forgery.

The Commissar General hands it to him.

FIRENZUOLA. Is the Bellarmine signature genuine?

SCHEINER, *examining it.* It does seem to be his handwriting. I don't understand.

GALILEO. But I do. The official minutes are inaccurate and defamatory!

SCHEINER, *quietly.* I formally request that Galilei be asked to withdraw.

FIRENZUOLA. Would you step outside for a moment, Professor?

He does so, with Castelli.

SCHEINER. The whole thing is now quite clear. Bellarmine was in his dotage, and Galileo got him to sign a document he didn't even read.

CARDINAL 1. Thus compounding his own crime. . . .

CARDINAL 2. By adding forgery to disobedience!

CARDINAL 3. Yes, that's *obviously* what happened.

CARDINAL 4. But then we don't know, do we, actually?

CARDINAL 5. No, suppose this document really was approved by Bellarmine?

CARDINAL 1. How can we suppose a thing like that?!

CARDINAL 6. Well, if this document was really approved by Bellarmine, then not only was Galileo not guilty of forgery; he would not be guilty of disobedience either.

CARDINAL 2. Which side are you on?

CARDINAL 1. We're here to find this man guilty, not hold student debates on the English model!

CARDINAL 2. The Protestant model!

Pause.

CARDINAL 6. I wonder if our true objective should not be stated thus. *At all costs avoid a public crisis. One Giordano Bruno was enough.*

More than enough. For an *auto da fe* which was supposed to deter heretics and help us only aroused indignation among heretics and made us repellent. Today, certainly, such an execution would serve only the Lutherans. If I am right, what follows? That, instead of making the name of Galilei a rallying point for our enemies, we should come only to conclusions which he himself will voluntarily accept.

CARDINAL 1. In which statement do we not read the fine Roman hand of Urban VIII?

CARDINAL 6. Can I not agree with my pope? No vows of absolute obedience limit *my* choice!

CARDINAL 2. That is an insult to the Society of Jesus!

CARDINAL 3. It certainly is!

FIRENZUOLA. Order, my lords! Cardinal Lucignano's point is well taken. Just as we should not be fighting each other, so also we should not be fighting Galilei.

CARDINAL 6. What we are apparently engaged in is a prize fight of which Galilei has won the first round.

CARDINAL 5. It was a mistake to urge an offence he couldn't possibly plead guilty to: writing a book on a topic he's been forbidden to mention!

CARDINAL 4. Besides, his version of what happened had Bellarmine's signature on it. Father Scheiner's had not.

SCHEINER. Are you insinuating that—

FIRENZUOLA. Cardinal Gorazio, you are out of order. My lords, you are here to judge Galilei, not each other.

CARDINAL 4, *pouting*. Well, well, ancient Rome had emperors, modern Rome has commissars. Tell us what to think, Firenzuola, tell us what to think!

FIRENZUOLA. Well, my dear Cardinal, would you have Galilei give the signal for protest and revolt to his admirers throughout Christendom?

CARDINAL 4. Of course not.

FIRENZUOLA. What is the injunction Galileo admits receiving, Father Scheiner?

SCHEINER. An order stating that he must not *defend* the forbidden views.

FIRENZUOLA. We have to concede, my lords, that he is licensed to *mention* the forbidden views. We do not have to concede that he may *defend* them. Very well, Father Scheiner will present the evidence that he has indeed defended them; and Galilei will be forced to agree. We can then ban the book *with his blessing*.

CARDINAL 1. Well, let's see if this works.

CARDINAL 3. Scheiner will find a way if anyone can.

CARDINAL 2. He certainly will.

FIRENZUOLA, *to secretary*. Ask Galilei to return.

SECRETARY, *in doorway*. Professor Galilei.

The professor returns with Castelli.

FIRENZUOLA. Father Scheiner, have you read Galilei's manuscript?

SCHEINER. Yes, Father Commissar.

FIRENZUOLA. Tell the tribunal whether Galilei has not only mentioned but also defended the forbidden view of the universe.

SCHEINER. I have made notes on that.

FIRENZUOLA. Read them.

CARDINAL 4. How long is this going to take? Some of us have appointments.

SCHEINER. Oh, about two hours.

CARDINAL 5. Two hours? What do you take us for?

CARDINAL 3. Sh, sh, sh. Sordi, let's show that English virtue shall we? What's it called—tolerance?

CARDINAL 1. Go on, Scheiner.

SCHEINER, *looks to Firenzuola. Firenzuola nods*. Very well. *He reads.* "Does Galilei teach the forbidden view? What is teaching? asks Saint Augustine, and answers, it is to communicate knowledge. Does Galilei communicate the knowledge of the forbidden view? He does. See pages 4 through 53, 72 through 96, 113 through 147, 196 through. . . ."

He continues in this vein for more than an hour.

". . . To summarize, the knowledge of the forbidden view is therefore communicated on a sum total of 364 pages. Nor is that all. Saint Thomas Aquinas states that a teacher indicates both his own approval of the doctrine taught and his desire that others should accept it. Such approval and such desire are clearly indicated on pages 33, 47, 68, 89, 113. . . .

He continues in this vein for more than another hour.

". . . To summarize, approval of the forbidden view and a desire for others to accept it is clearly indicated on a sum total of 166 pages. The fact that the book is written in Italian, not the customary Latin, must also be urged as evidence that Professor Galilei wished to ingratiate himself with the public."

FIRENZUOLA. Any comments, Professor Galilei?

GALILEO. Am I supposed to remember all those page numbers? Father Scheiner has been talking for two and a half hours.

CARDINAL 3. Father Commissar, if the Holy Office is to be insulted, I move that the session be adjourned.

FIRENZUOLA. Galilei, tell the tribunal if Father Scheiner's report is just or unjust.

GALILEO. I can make an uninterrupted rejoinder?

FIRENZUOLA. Of course.

GALILEO, *after a pause.* As Father Scheiner spoke I was reminded of Roman Law—in which the omission of relevant truths coupled with the cunning suggestion of untruths constitutes lying. At no point did Father Scheiner weigh the pro and con; at no point did he let the relevant fact and falsehood confront each other; at no point did he attempt to measure differing degrees of relevance. But let us forget Father Scheiner, even if that will be difficult, and let us remember Cardinal Bellarmine, whose advice I have either flouted or not flouted. He "advised" me not to "defend" the "erroneous" view of Copernicus. But I don't believe that view to *be* erroneous. The church, in its infallible wisdom, has never proclaimed it so; has never made this a matter of dogma. Even in the opinion of the church, therefore, such a view can only be erroneous till it is proved correct. I did not "defend" this view. I spent long years proving it correct; so that it would no longer be held "erroneous"; after which no one could disapprove if I taught it.

Father Scheiner jumps up.

FIRENZUOLA. One moment, Scheiner. Cardinal Silotti has the floor.

CARDINAL 1. Has your secretary taken all this down, Firenzuola?

FIRENZUOLA, *giving the secretary a glance.* Oh yes, of course.

CARDINAL 1. That is all I care to say at this time.

FIRENZUOLA. Cardinal Girardi?

A moment in the trial of Galileo which does not correspond to any moment in the present play, nor perhaps to any moment in the historical record, engraved by G. Harrubini and L. Paradisi, in 1857, after a painting by Christiano Banti of the same year. (*Bettmann Archive*)

CARDINAL 2. Galilei, if you publish these . . . so-called proofs, then you *are* teaching them.

GALILEO. But first, before they are published, you yourselves have the chance to judge if the proofs are better than "so-called" or not. If you should judge that they are, then I would be authorized to teach them.

CARDINAL 3. But then you are teaching *us* in advance of such judgment.

GALILEO. How am I to present a subject without teaching it? Would you have me present truths as untruths?

FIRENZUOLA. I must disallow these questions, Galilei. The prisoner does not cross-examine his judges.

GALILEO, *shrugging*. What does he do?

FIRENZUOLA. He gives his version of the truth.

SCHEINER. If he has what it takes.

GALILEO. Hm?

SCHEINER. He has what it takes to denounce others as liars. Dare he reveal what he himself holds to be true?

GALILEO. Good point, Scheiner. How about it, Castelli? Dare I? Frankly, my lords, I had not thought it would be necessary. But if it is . . . why not? In a sense you already know. This is a charade we have been playing. I will end it.
Short pause.
What Bellarmine told me was that the truth is old and the truth is known. In my field, that of physical science, we call truth "new" because it is not known but is in the process of being discovered. What passes for the known is progressively revealed to be error. Do you see what happens if you come into my field with the pre-conceptions of Bellarmine? To him, precisely the new is the erroneous and so must not be taught. We reply that unless we can mention it, present it, and to that extent defend it, we cannot establish that it is true. You see then what Bellarmine proposed to me? The Copernican view was new and therefore, as far as he was concerned, wrong; but if I wanted to spend my life trying to prove it right, that was my affair. I risked failure. A double failure. Should the doctrine prove false, I would have willfully spent my life defending what I was advised not to defend because it was known to be

false all along. But what else could I do? To me, Catholicism is true. I believe that, being dedicated to truth, the church must and will accept *anything* that can be proved true. Some truths are more important, no doubt, than the truths of physics, but, for a Catholic physicist, this can hardly mean that, in physics, the church prefers falsehood to truth. *Pause.* Bellarmine, God rest his soul, is dead. The church lives. It is the church in which I place my hopes. My church *cannot* be hostile to "new" truth in physical science, for truth in physical science *is* "new." My church will be hospitable to scientific discovery. I appeal from Bellarmine—to you, my lords. *Silence.*

CARDINAL 5. I'm flabbergasted.

CARDINAL 4. Did I hear you right, Galilei? You are asking not only to be let off but celebrated as the hero of the occasion?

GALILEO. I am asking that we drop all pretense, admit that what is at stake is our view of the universe, and accept the view which has been proved true.

CARDINAL 5. You would turn the tables on us!

GALILEO. Cardinal Lucignano, I appeal to you.

CARDINAL 6. I'm afraid, Galilei, you have now passed the bounds. I too would have to concede that your book must be banned.

CARDINAL 1, *to Firenzuola.* I request that the prisoner be asked to withdraw.

FIRENZUOLA. The guards will escort you to your quarters, Galilei. *Galileo and Castelli leave.*

CARDINAL 1. The book, says Cardinal Lucignano, must be banned. What triviality is this? Galilei has come right out with it at long last! Father Scheiner is to be congratulated on prying this statement loose. Do you realize, my lords, what it amounts to?

CARDINAL 2. An admission.

CARDINAL 3. An outright admission of guilt.

CARDINAL 1. Yes. And what guilt?

CARDINAL 3. Disobeying Bellarmine.

CARDINAL 2. Disobedience—the sin of Adam.

CARDINAL 1. Adam and Eve were guilty of a single act of disobedience, over in a moment, but this man persisted in his sin for many years—

only to end, here, today, with the Holy Office itself as witnesses, condoning his disobedience, nay, even asking holy church to sanction it!

FIRENZUOLA. Are you asking the tribunal to take a new position, Your Eminence?

CARDINAL 1. Most definitely. We came here to judge a book. We are now compelled to judge a man.

CARDINAL 3. Galilei used the phrase, *he consults his notes,* "even in the opinion of the church." As if church doctrine were no more than personal preference!

CARDINAL 2. To be pitted against the preferences of Professor Galilei!

CARDINAL 1, *definitively.* Compounding disobedience with defiance, this man has proved himself an out-and-out heretic.

CARDINAL 3. That is exactly it.

CARDINAL 2. And must be punished as such.

FIRENZUOLA. To be specific, my lords. . . .

CARDINAL 1. "Specific!" Since when do commissars talk schoolteachers? The Holy Inquisition has made its presence felt throughout Europe by one thing and one thing only!

CARDINAL 2. The stake!

CARDINAL 6. I object. The stake is for heretics. The Copernican view of the universe—though an error—has never yet been pronounced a heresy.

CARDINAL 1. Is this the Holy Office or a theology seminar? How many of the Inquisition's victims have been openly committed to a declared heresy?

CARDINAL 3. They're far too smart.

CARDINAL 2. Like this man before us now.

CARDINAL 1. Need I remind you, Lucignano, heresy today is not a matter of doctrine only: it is a *spirit* that bloweth where the Devil listeth by the agency of unquiet souls spreading disaffection as dungflies spread disease.

CARDINAL 6. Even so, it has to be proved, by overt acts, that they have done this. Galilei has written an unpublished book that has been submitted to us alone—

CARDINAL 1. Giving us the chance to *prevent* catastrophe.

CARDINAL 6. Is that a Christian approach?

CARDINAL 1. Who was it that said to think adultery was to commit it? Our Lord Himself. It behoves us, therefore, to see into men's thoughts in advance of "overt acts." See into them, and punish them. *Sharply.* The three Jesuit members of this tribunal demand the death of Galilei.

FIRENZUOLA. Cardinal Gorazio?

CARDINAL 4. I agree to that.

CARDINAL 5. And I.

> *Silence.*

FIRENZUOLA. Cardinal Lucignano?

> *Silence.*

Unanimity being lacking, may I make a suggestion?

CARDINAL 1. What is it?

FIRENZUOLA. When there is no clear mandate from the tribunal, the Inquisition has a way of securing one from the accused.

CARDINAL 3. Extracting a confession?

CARDINAL 1. Galilei's present stance does not suggest that he would give you one.

CARDINAL 2. Though we have seen these "stances" crumble often enough.

CARDINAL 3. Under torture.

CARDINAL 6. I will not agree to the use of torture in this case.

FIRENZUOLA. Nor would I propose it. I would propose only to talk to Galilei—alone.

CARDINAL 6. What will you have him confess? This is not a man who will put himself in the wrong to save his skin.

FIRENZUOLA. That is why it will be advisable only to ask him to admit that he did disobey Bellarmine. And, at that, unintentionally—not by malice but through vanity.

SCHEINER. A venial sin! A nothing! Why, he has already confessed more than that before this tribunal!

CARDINAL 1, *softly.* Gently, Scheiner. *Scheiner recognizes that this is an order.* Lucignano, do you agree to Firenzuola's plan?

CARDINAL 6. Very well.

FIRENZUOLA. Then I have your authorization, my lords? *Silence.* Good. We reconvene tomorrow morning. I shall visit Galilei this afternoon.

The image of Galileo in prison fascinated the historical painters of the nineteenth century. Here are two examples. First, an engraving by John Sartain from *Eclectic Magazine* (1853) after a painting by J. A. Laurent, 1822; second, an engraving by F. L. Meyer from *Portfolio Magazine* (1878) from a painting by Karl von Piloty, 1862. (*Bettmann Archive*)

Scene Seven

A FRIENDLY COMMISSAR

Palace of the Inquisition. Galileo's quarters. Guards in the entrance hall. Castelli is eating lunch from a tray.

GUARD. The Commissar General.
  Firenzuola enters.
FIRENZUOLA, *to Castelli.* I wish to see the professor alone.
  Castelli goes out to a back room where, we can assume, Galileo has been resting. Enter Galileo. The two men stand facing each other.
FIRENZUOLA. Please be seated, Professor. *Galileo sits.* A private conference between the two of us has been deemed desirable before the tribunal reconvenes. Is that agreeable to you?
GALILEO. Has nothing been decided yet?
FIRENZUOLA. I represent the Inquisition. May I use *our* method of procedure?
GALILEO. By all means.
FIRENZUOLA. I shall begin by sounding you out a little. What is your own sense of the situation?
GALILEO. Do I know what the situation now is?
FIRENZUOLA. Of the situation . . . as it has developed during the hearing. How would you say you were doing?
GALILEO. Not too badly. I nailed down the main weaknesses in Scheiner's position.
FIRENZUOLA. You maintained—correct me if I'm wrong—that he is a liar. Even a forger.
GALILEO. I *proved* those things.
FIRENZUOLA. And proof lies very near to your heart, isn't that true?
GALILEO. That is very true.

FIRENZUOLA. Would you expect Scheiner to enjoy being exposed?

GALILEO. No.

FIRENZUOLA. Yet you needed him. No one but he had read your book.

GALILEO. The others *could* read my book.

FIRENZUOLA. And understand it?

GALILEO. I could help them understand it.

FIRENZUOLA. Between now and tomorrow's session?

GALILEO. The world has waited centuries for these truths. The tribunal could wait another week or two.

FIRENZUOLA. And in that spirit you have appealed from Scheiner to the six cardinals?

GALILEO. Yes.

FIRENZUOLA. Three of whom, like Scheiner himself, are members of the Society of Jesus. *Silence.* Any comment?

GALILEO. Your own irony is a comment. But not mine.

FIRENZUOLA. You wouldn't, of course, have made this appeal if you didn't think it could succeed?

GALILEO. I wouldn't. No.

FIRENZUOLA. What are—or were—its chances of success?

GALILEO. Oh, about fifty-fifty.

FIRENZUOLA. Yes?

GALILEO. Lucignano's friendly, isn't he? Gorazio and Sordi will jog along behind him, I should think. That's half the tribunal.

FIRENZUOLA. You need five votes.

GALILEO. Are you assuming that the individual Jesuits don't think for themselves?

FIRENZUOLA. What would *you* assume?

GALILEO. That they have to. Because they respect themselves. And their order knows about science. . . . They are not inquisitors, they are Catholics, Father Commissar!

FIRENZUOLA. Ah, then you have a *better* than fifty-fifty chance?

GALILEO. Maybe. If this must be regarded as a gamble. I'd have said *faith* had something to do with it. You know, the faith which can move mountains.

FIRENZUOLA. Very good, very good. I am not employing our inquisitorial method to torment you. Merely to bring the truth home to you. You have certainly brought home to me your illusion. *Quietly.* Galilei, after you left this morning, the tribunal dismissed your appeal. Unanimously.

GALILEO. What? My book is to be banned?

FIRENZUOLA. Which was inevitable, as I told you in advance.

GALILEO. The tribunal will not even entertain the *possibility* that the earth moves round the sun?

FIRENZUOLA. Will not even entertain the possibility.

Pause.

GALILEO. It's unbelievable.

FIRENZUOLA. Tell me *why* it is unbelievable.

GALILEO. Because what my book provides is not opinion but proof.

FIRENZUOLA. Proof of what?

GALILEO. Of the truth. Obviously.

FIRENZUOLA. The truth. Obviously. Is what is "obvious" to Galilei "obvious" to a tribunal of the Holy Office? Could it be?

GALILEO. Be plain with me, Father Commissar. Proving things true has been my life's business, my personal vocation. Proving certain things true to the Holy Office has occupied me continuously for over fifteen years. The results are in that manuscript. Now, if truth did not interest the Holy Office, what would that show?

FIRENZUOLA. What *would* it show?

GALILEO. A career, a whole life based on a total misunderstanding. A life thrown away. Wasted.

FIRENZUOLA. I should not have enjoyed formulating those phrases.

GALILEO. Then it is so? There is no interest in truth here in Rome *at all?*

FIRENZUOLA. I am not trying to instruct you but to help you to . . . certain conclusions.

GALILEO, *suddenly.* Do you think you're God? But God could never be indifferent to truth. *You* can? Firenzuola, you're a person, aren't you, let me address you as such. Are you totally unconcerned with truth? *Silence.* Then what *are* you concerned with?

FIRENZUOLA, *unruffled.* What *is* a Commissar concerned with?

GALILEO, *bitterly.* Power. Just naked power. I suppose that's what you are trying to tell me.

FIRENZUOLA. Let's say administration. A Commissar has very little power. He does what he's told.

GALILEO. By the cardinals. Are you saying they're a lot of power-hungry politicians?

FIRENZUOLA. Heaven forbid! I've got you too excited, Galilei. Let me ask you an academic question. What is a church?

GALILEO. What?

FIRENZUOLA. Not what does it stand for. What is it?

GALILEO. An institution, of course—

FIRENZUOLA. An institution. Among other institutions of this world. Matching itself against other institutions of this world. Matching itself as to what? As to power. Its power against theirs. Or it will no longer exist in this world. What way out is there, except to exist only in other worlds? But the Catholic Church was placed *here* by Christ Himself. Upon this rock. Upon this earth.

GALILEO. I'm naive in politics, the point is not new. But how, in God's holy name, is the church threatened by wholly unpolitical activities such as mine? How is it threatened by the motion of the earth around the sun?

FIRENZUOLA. I think Bellarmine must have explained that years ago.

GALILEO. He said all new views were wrong.

FIRENZUOLA. Would that we still had his simplicity! *Pause.* The church is a fabric of traditions, nothing else. None of these traditions must be broken or the fabric as whole would fray, wear through, disintegrate. Now, if Bellarmine could feel that a generation ago, how much more strongly must any good Catholic feel it today! Protestant power was *not* stopped, as Bellarmine hoped. Throughout Central and Northern Europe, a so-called war of religion has been raging fifteen years, and no end in sight. Not just that, but—

GALILEO, *stopping him rudely.* Yes, yes! *Silence.* But this preoccupation of yours with power and the struggle for power, this disregard of truth and the struggle for truth, this is just your viewpoint, Firenzuola, an inquisitor's viewpoint. The cardinals of the Catholic Church could not, dare not, permit themselves—

FIRENZUOLA, *cutting in just as abruptly.* You appealed to them from Scheiner. Would you now appeal to them from me?

GALILEO. Yes. I reject this "private conference." *Much louder.* Let me go back before the cardinals. Let me set my proofs before the tribunal.

FIRENZUOLA, *gently.* Very good. I can now complete my report. This morning, Galilei, five of the six cardinals voted for your execution. *Pause.* By burning. *Pause.* At the stake. If, like Scheiner, I am suspected of lying, you may send Castelli to check.

GALILEO. Burning at the stake!

FIRENZUOLA. The verdict was halted by a single opposing vote; but till tomorrow morning only. Hence the decisive importance of this meeting this afternoon.

GALILEO. Not burning at the stake!

FIRENZUOLA. I see you have believed me.
    Silence.

GALILEO, *suddenly.* I have been living in a fool's paradise.

FIRENZUOLA. Had I said so myself, at the outset, you wouldn't have believed me.

GALILEO. My whole life *has* been based on a misunderstanding. All these efforts, these years, *have* been wasted.

FIRENZUOLA. And there is very little time left.

GALILEO. For what?

FIRENZUOLA. I have been cruel. But for a purpose. As things stand you will be condemned to death tomorrow. You do not have to be.

GALILEO. What are you talking about?

FIRENZUOLA. Even as the captive Arab king can escape the stake by a last-minute genuflection before the cross, so you can escape it by one small token gesture of submission.

GALILEO. What?

FIRENZUOLA. Read this. *Hands him a scroll.*

GALILEO, *reading tonelessly.* "I, Galileo Galilei, do hereby confess to the sin of disobedience, which sin, however, was committed unintentionally, in zeal prompted by idle vanity, and not in malice as an enemy of Holy Church."
    Silence.
    And in this way my lifelong attempt to change the church's mind is abandoned forever.

FIRENZUOLA. As you have just demonstrated, your attempt to change the church's mind has definitively *failed*.

GALILEO. Definitively? Are *you* the church?

FIRENZUOLA. The Holy Office speaks for the church; the Holy Inquisition acts for it.

GALILEO. No. No, no, no! I had heard the Jesuits were slippery, I had heard the Inquisition was arbitrary, and had not dared to believe it. It's true. But they are not the church. And a final appeal still remains open, the appeal that all Catholics may make when others have failed.

FIRENZUOLA. The appeal to the pope? You have already appealed to him.

GALILEO. The book was snatched from his grasp by the Inquisition. As a good Catholic, I demand the right to present my case to him in person.

FIRENZUOLA. Today? At a couple of hours' notice?

GALILEO. That is for you to say. *I* don't mind if the tribunal does not meet tomorrow!

FIRENZUOLA. The pope cannot commute a sentence passed by the Holy Office.

GALILEO. Will the Holy Office pass sentence if the pope agrees to state in public what he has already conceded in private?

FIRENZUOLA. Namely?

GALILEO. That the earth moves round the sun.

FIRENZUOLA. That, my dear Galilei, would be more than his triple crown is worth.

GALILEO, *loudly*. I believe in my Barberini! I have the right to see him! *Silence*.

FIRENZUOLA. I shall try to get you an audience for this evening.

Portrait of Pope Urban VIII, formerly Cardinal Barberini, as engraved after a painting by Simon Vouet (1590–1649). (*Bettmann Archive*)

Scene Eight

A SINCERE STATESMAN

The Vatican. A modest audience chamber. Pope Urban VIII is seated, not on a throne, but on a straightbacked chair. If Firenzuola is an administrator, Urban is every inch the statesman, the kind that lies awake nights. Reality gnaws him, and he owes his success in life not least to his conspicuous and authentic sincerity. Sincerity such as his has a function that does not go unappreciated. It gives the impression that something is to be hoped from the established order; and through such men this order seeks, if not the realization of the hopes concerned, at least a modus vivendi. *Firenzuola and Castelli are also present, as Galileo winds up his presentation.*

GALILEO. . . . Put it then, that, in my human weakness, I have been unable to persuade the tribunal of the truth of these views. In the light of this unhappy fact, your own prior knowledge of the truth gains a unique importance. For you are in a position to see for yourself that a condemnation of it at this time would set back science 200 years throughout Catholic Europe, thus giving the lead to Protestant Germany and England, not to belabor the point that for You, Your Holiness, truth needs no testimonial but is itself of God.

Pause.

POPE, *nervously.* That's the plea, then, is it? You've finished?

GALILEO. Yes, Your Holiness.

POPE. Never become pope, Firenzuola, or these things will happen to *you.* An hour ago We were asked to stop the war in Germany. Now We are asked to open up a few new worlds. Can't you take a hint, Galileo? Can't you see the writing on the wall? No one kneels in the snow before the pope these days. They file their petitions with the cardinals and the commissars.

GALILEO. I have been learning that. But I have come to you just because you are not one of these . . . men of power.

POPE. My dear Galileo, how should We have more power than the men of power?

GALILEO. Because there is more than "power" in this world, in our church. Because people respect you and your office. Because even cardinals and commissars would think twice before flouting you.

POPE. There is nothing We can do.

GALILEO. I could write on a piece of paper, "The earth revolves about the sun, as was discovered by Copernicus, and proved by Galileo." And you could sign it.

POPE. Are you out of your mind?

GALILEO. Have *you* read my proofs?

POPE. No.

GALILEO. Then you must, Your Holiness. At once. Everything hinges on that.

POPE. My dear fellow, nothing hinges on that. We were "persuaded," as far as that goes, years ago. It does not follow that We are in a position to favor such views now.

GALILEO. I am not asking for favor. Only for you to state in public what in private you know to be true.

POPE. Galileo, enough is enough. We agreed to this audience at two hours' notice and in the evening of all times, not to help the universe but to help you: the universe must wait till We have halfway settled the German problem. The father commissar has shown us the confession he wrote for you. We shall simply add our prayers to his. Show him the document again, Firenzuola, would you? Read it again, Galileo, and this time—sign it.

GALILEO. Adding your prayers to his? You want me to . . . ? You too?

POPE. Sign it. Sign it. We might add that Cardinal Lucignano is also backing this little plot; it is the only way to save your life.
Pause.

GALILEO. I am going to have to see Your Holiness alone.

90

FIRENZUOLA. That is against protocol, Galilei. His Holiness *never*—

GALILEO, *loudly.* I will not sign any confession! I refuse!

POPE. Leave us, Firenzuola, Castelli. We shall grant his request.

> *They leave.*
>
> So His Holiness is alone. Does it help?
>
> *Pause.*

GALILEO. I think I understand. This is the only way you can save a life. But I am old. More important to me than continued life is the knowledge that the life I have already had has not been lived in vain.

POPE. But of course it hasn't! The list of your achievements—

GALILEO. I have lived for one truth. To put it through. To convince the church of it.

POPE. It has been explained to you—

GALILEO. *When* will the church be convinced? Just answer me that. *If not now, when?*

POPE. Galileo—

GALILEO. *You* are convinced already. Were convinced long ago. Today, as far as public announcements go, your hands are tied. I understand that too. I resent it, but I understand. You cannot speak in front of the others. So I asked them to leave. Speak to *me*. No one is listening, and I swear before your God and mine that I will never repeat what you now say. *How long do you expect to keep up this pretence?*

POPE. Pretence? But, my dear Galileo—

GALILEO. Yes, pretence. That the sun goes round the earth. For you it is a pretence. You're forgetting I know that! How long can you keep it up? *When, when* will you come out for the truth?

POPE, *trembling.* Galileo, I cannot allow this interview to continue! You are insulting me! No good can come of that!

GALILEO. Insulting you? Just the contrary! I grant that you have no choice, no power, that you must do what you are pushed into doing, that it's the cardinals that rule, the Jesuits, the inquisitors—

POPE. Am I some petty politician that I must do what I think is wrong for the good of my career?

GALILEO. For your decision you gave political reasons, and political reasons only.

POPE. My conscience is clear, let me tell you, my conscience is clear.

GALILEO. Huh? Then you *will* come out for the truth? Yes! You *have* to!

POPE. Good God, man, can't you conceive of any other reason for keeping quiet? Other than politics, other than sheer opportunism?

GALILEO. You didn't give me any. Nobody has given me any!

Pause.

POPE. True. We cannot give you the real reason.

GALILEO. You *can* let me die.

Pause.

POPE, *almost in a whisper.* Then let me avail myself, after all, of the secrecy—the secrecy before our God—which you offered, and utter behind these closed doors that which till now we have not told a living soul. . . . What is it, this older view of the universe that the church accepts? A fiction that "saves the appearances." If the universe was created for the single purpose of being inhabited by men, science must content itself with showing how this purpose has been carried out. It could hardly be carried out by stars outside the range of man's natural eyesight. Therefore, there *are* no such stars. The earth *is* in the center. Believing these things, the intellect is quieted, and men may turn to the more important matter of their souls and the salvation thereof.

GALILEO. But you know the answer to all this.

POPE. At one time, yes, I was willing to begin at the other end, not asking how things can be fitted into the Christian story, but asking how they are *in mere fact,* as seen through telescopes and measured with no further end in view. But don't you see where that leads, Galileo? To a question not to be asked: the question whether the Christian story can be fitted into the facts.

GALILEO. The facts are not all known but—

POPE. Since the facts are as yet unknown, it follows that anything, *anything,* can turn out to be true. Giordano Bruno suggested that this universe is not the only one there is! Suggested that there are an infinite number of others! Suppose *that* should turn out to be true! What happens to the Christian doctrine of God and His only beloved Son? Did He send out an infinite number of only beloved sons—or the same son an infinite number of times—a celestial travelling salesman, selling an infinite number of parables and ending on an infinite number of crosses?

Silence.

GALILEO. Still, *if* it were true, you would have to *acknowledge* that it was true.

POPE. What? No, no, no! Haven't you followed me, even now? I would have to *refuse* to acknowledge that it was true!

GALILEO. Don't you care? Don't you give a good God damn *what* the truth is?

POPE. Not a good God damn! Not a good God damn! Let me employ your blasphemous phrase. For what I care about—what is *in* my care, entrusted to my care, by Him who damns and saves—is of greater import.

GALILEO. And what may that be?

POPE. The welfare of my people. The welfare of my Catholic people—in this world and the next. To Hell—yes, to *Hell*—with truth! For who knows if our poor notions of it, changing as they do like the colors of the chameleon, are not *from* Hell? One thing I do know: the people—the community of believers—are my sheep. I am their shepherd. *Silence.* Let me, in the secrecy of this encounter, admit the irrelevance of all the arguments publicly used against you. In consideration of the supreme relevance of our secret, you as a good Catholic will now sign this confession.

Silence. Then Galileo lets out a great cry of pain. The pope turns pale.

GALILEO. Don't blanch, Barberini, I wasn't even listening to you. Oh yes, I heard you, but as your voice droned on, do you know what happened? My whole life passed in review before me. All the years I have willed one thing, and everyone urged me on. I would discover certain things, and everyone would be grateful. My mother, my schoolteachers, my professors, my students, even, it seemed at times, princes, churchmen, the whole established order, the whole world would be grateful. The church—and the church was and is my world—would be grateful. There were set-

backs, yes. I was warned. But I refused to accept setbacks. I refused to take no for an answer, true to type in this also: always the go-getter, the top boy of the class, the gilded youth, the acknowledged genius. Well, here the road ends. Here the success story stops. For here I sit with the top man of all—Christ's deputy on earth—a pope, at that, by no means to be despised, one of the best, and my friend, the only pope in history, perhaps, who would ever have understood what a scientist was talking about—and he is sending me a message I can only translate into these words: *You talk of truth but you have spent your whole life on an illusion. You who live your life in the conscious possession of genius are, in the actual living of that life, a dunce! An idiot!!*
Silence.

POPE. You leave me with no alternative but to turn you back to the tender mercies of my cardinals. Firenzuola!

FIRENZUOLA, *reentering.* Yes, Your Holiness?

POPE. He will not sign.

GALILEO. Huh? You want me to sign that thing? Give it here. What difference does it make? What difference does anything make now?
Sobbing, he signs the confession.

Another artist's image of Galileo before the Inquisition, painted in 1847 by J. N. Robert-Fleury, and now in the Louvre. (*Bettmann Archive*)

97

Scene Nine

ON RECANTATIONS

Palace of the Inquisition, as in Scene Six. All are in their places as before. Firenzuola is just finishing the reading of Galileo's confession.

FIRENZUOLA. ". . . Hereby humbly confess the sin of disobedience, which sin, however, was committed unintentionally, in zeal prompted by idle vanity, and not maliciously as an enemy of Holy Church. Signed by me, this 18th day of June, 1633, Galileo Galilei."

Pause.

CARDINAL 4. Well, what do we do now? Pass a vote of thanks to Firenzuola?

CARDINAL 5. To line up an evening audience with the pope on two hours' notice is probably the most remarkable feat of practical acumen in the history of the church.

CARDINAL 6. May I remind you, my lords, that a man's fate is in your hands? The death sentence having been canceled we are faced, I take it, with the sacred obligation of meeting penitence with forgiveness.

CARDINAL 1. I beg to differ. We are faced with the sacred obligation of defining the offence and imposing appropriate penalities.

CARDINAL 6. May I suggest that the offence is defined in the confession we have just heard—written as it was, by the commissar general and signed in the presence of the Holy Father?

CARDINAL 3. The pope has no jurisdiction here.

CARDINAL 4. It is still the case that penalties have to be decided on—and approved by at least five of us.

CARDINAL 3. Well, it's clear that the book cannot be published in any shape or form.

CARDINAL 2. Well, even you agree to that, don't you, Lucignano?

CARDINAL 6. Alas, I see no way out.

CARDINAL 4. So that's about it, hm?

CARDINAL 3. I suppose so.

CARDINAL 1. One moment. Are you proposing, my lords, to let Galilei go scot free?

CARDINAL 6. That *would* be forgiveness.

CARDINAL 1. I was addressing myself to Sordi and Gorazio.

CARDINAL 4. Well, as I said yesterday, we have appointments.

CARDINAL 3. We just wanted to get the whole thing over with.

CARDINAL 1. I see. But first I want you to hear a statement I asked Father Scheiner to prepare.

Here Galileo begins to show signs of life, but only, so far, in exchanging a look with Castelli. Cardinal 1 looks to Firenzuola to give the signal.

FIRENZUOLA. Father Scheiner.

SCHEINER. During the early stages of the hearing, Galilei pleaded total innocence. If there was any guilt at all, he was at pains to attach it to my humble self. Which would have little importance, except that I was the main source of evidence against him. The thesis of the *poisoned source* being not only useful but *necessary* to him, I was guilty of mendacity, even of forgery. If he was innocent, his accuser had to be guilty. If he spoke truth, his accuser had to be a liar. But now Galilei has pleaded guilty and the positions are reversed. He is guilty, his accuser is innocent. He lies; and it is not the accuser who is lying. I therefore come before you in a new role, my lords: the accuser whose credentials are not in question. In this role, I would call the tribunal's attention to the *character* of Galilei's confession. Let us dismiss at once the qualification— that he didn't intend to be guilty, etcetera. Who does? What sin does he confess to? Disobedience. Now those of you who wish to favor the sinner may urge forgiveness. Those of you who have pressing appointments elsewhere may favor getting rid of the case as quickly as possible on any terms. But to the others of you— and indeed to *all* of you really, since no appointments are all *that* pressing, and "forgiveness" is not what the Inquisition is really all about—I say: if the prisoner is guilty of disobedience, as he attests, what follows? If he did disobey Bellarmine after all, we are back, are we not, with the account of things which I gave yesterday morning when the professor tried to discredit me as a liar and cheat. If the original offence was disobedience, then what ensued was consistent defiance of the church over a period of many years culminating in a brazen attempt to have you, my lords, set your seal of approval upon the whole iniquitous adventure. Five of you judged that the man was a heretic. This judgment has now been confirmed by the prisoner himself.

Silence.

CARDINAL 6. Are you suggesting that he be punished . . . as my five colleagues yesterday decided?

CARDINAL 1. No, no. In any case, Father Scheiner is here in an advisory capacity. We, we—

CARDINAL 6. We?

CARDINAL 1. The three Jesuits on the tribunal naturally meet in caucus between sessions.

CARDINAL 6. Naturally. And with Scheiner present?

CARDINAL 1. Of course. And therefore Scheiner will not—any more than the rest of us—ask for a death sentence. But as for setting the prisoner scot free, that is out of the question.

CARDINAL 5. Then you have a counter-proposal?

CARDINAL 1. A very precise one.

CARDINAL 4. Let's hear it then.

CARDINAL 1. That the book is to be suppressed is already agreed. Next: the heretic Galileo Galilei must be isolated from the community. A condition of *quarantine* is indicated. Such an infection must not be allowed to spread. If not in jail, this man must be under life-long house arrest.

Again, communication between Galileo and Castelli, though only to the extent that Galileo seems to be awaking more and more from his previous torpor. Castelli is excited.

CARDINAL 5. You're right, of course, my lord.

CARDINAL 4. I agree—without hesitation.

CARDINAL 1. Third and last, the confession just made being inadequate and misleading, for the reasons Father Scheiner has given, there must be another confession—and no little private affair either, but before the whole world—that closes up all loopholes.

FIRENZUOLA. Loopholes? I wrote the confession, my lord, and left no holes—unless it was one through which, with God's help, the soul of Galilei might still creep to salvation.

CARDINAL 3. Even though the same loophole might serve the Devil's purposes?

CARDINAL 2. Might serve to spread this man's heresy throughout Christendom?

FIRENZUOLA. I do not follow you now.

CARDINAL 3. Then it devolves upon the Holy Office to recall the Inquisition itself to duty.

CARDINAL 2. Exactly. Galilei confessed a venial sin, vanity, instead of a deadly one, pride. Excessive zeal is all it amounted to, the sin of enthusiastic adolescents. But enthusiasm for what? For an error. Of that there is no hint in your confession, commissar general.

CARDINAL 1. We therefore demand that, in the revised and public confession, the error be specified and denounced.

CARDINAL 6. I object. This is to ask Galilei to spit upon his own ideas, his whole life's work.

CARDINAL 3. Wouldn't you ask Satan to spit upon his own ideas, his whole life's work?

CARDINAL 2, *venomously.* The time has come to ignore you, Cardinal Lucignano. You are in a minority of one.

CARDINAL 6. Do the other five agree to that sentiment? *Looks are exchanged. No one says no.* Then there is nothing more I can do, Galilei. God have mercy on us all.

He leaves the room.

CARDINAL 1. Father Commissar, will you ask Father Scheiner to read the recantation.*

FIRENZUOLA. The revised confession?

CARDINAL 1. The recantation. With preamble and appendix.

---

* Actually, the church called it an abjuration. It is only popular tradition that Galileo "recanted." In matters like this, however, a playwright must follow popular tradition.

FIRENZUOLA. Father Scheiner.

SCHEINER. "Galileo Galilei, wearing the white shirt of penitence, shall so proceed through the public streets of Rome to the Convent of Santa Maria Sopra Minerva, and there, upon his knees before the Congregation of the Faithful, shall speak aloud the following words:

I, Galileo Galilei, do now with a sincere heart and unfeigned faith, abjure, detest, and curse the heretical belief that the earth moves round the sun, and do take my oath that never again will I speak, write or otherwise assert anything which might lend plausibility to this belief. Should anyone suspected of subscribing to this heretical belief be known to me I shall denounce him to this Holy Office in Rome or to the Inquisitor in whatsoever place I shall be. Appendix: This recantation, translated into foreign tongues, shall thereafter be read in every church in Christendom."

FIRENZUOLA. But, Father Scheiner—my lords—if this document is accepted, then mine was a decoy, a trap—

CARDINAL 2. Oh, come, Firenzuola, don't pretend you are above such things.

Pause.

FIRENZUOLA. The power is yours, my lords. But I cannot, any more than Cardinal Lucignano, share the responsibility. I hereby withdraw from this proceeding.

Exit Firenzuola.

CARDINAL 1, *without hesitation.* In the absence of the commissar general, Father Scheiner will preside.

SCHEINER, *taking Firenzuola's seat.* Is there now unanimity in the tribunal? Cardinal Gorazio?

CARDINAL 4. As far as I'm concerned.

CARDINAL 5. Yes, yes.

SCHEINER. Then our deliberations would seem to be at an end.

GALILEO. One moment. *Almost as if he were a forgotten figure in the proceeding, he arrests the attention of the tribunal with something of a start.* Weren't you expecting to hear from me?

CARDINAL 1. For what purpose?

SCHEINER, *gently.* The position you are in is well understood, Galilei.

GALILEO. The position I am in?

CARDINAL 4. In chess it is known as checkmate.

CARDINAL 5. That is true, Galilei. The game has been a long one. But it ended last night when His Holiness Pope Urban VIII refused you his support.

SCHEINER, *always quieter than the others.* For always you had gone over the head of your opponents. From the dean of your University—you recall *our* first meeting?—to the grand duke. From the grand duke to Bellarmine. From the Inquisition to the pope. Over the pope's head there is no one.

CARDINAL 5. Cardinal Gorazio and myself are even very sorry about it.

CARDINAL 4. We had no desire to make any trouble for you.

SCHEINER. Here is your signed confession. Here is the recantation. You will tear up the former and sign the latter.

Pause. Then Galileo walks over to Scheiner's table, takes the confession and tears it up. Pause.

SCHEINER. Which disposes of the confession. Now sign the recantation.

GALILEO, *picking up the recantation and looking at him.* Your account was very correct, Father Scheiner. I've been on your mind a lot during the past twenty years, haven't I? The dean, the grand duke, the Master of Controversial Questions, the pope, and "over the pope's head there is no one." After which you can ask me to do anything, and I'll do it. "Sign this confession." And I signed it.

SCHEINER. Indeed. And now the formality of replacing it with this one.

GALILEO. A formality, and all is over. *He looks at the cardinals.* Let me drink in the . . . peculiar feeling of . . . the moment before the moment. *Pointing to the recantation. Why* am I signing this, Scheiner?

SCHEINER. Because, at this point, no other course is open to you.

GALILEO. Except, of course, death—at the stake.

SCHEINER. You signed the confession to exclude *that* possibility.

GALILEO. I signed it because nothing mattered any more.

SCHEINER. Such are the rationalizations of cowardice.

The dialogue has been getting quieter and quieter as the two antagonists have talked less and less for the tribunal and more and more for each other. And now Galileo, who had walked away from Scheiner with the scroll bearing the recantation in his hand, returns and slaps him with it. Two sharp blows, one on each cheek. Scheiner jumps to his feet. The cardinals start to rise but sit again as Galileo takes over.

GALILEO, *continuing where he left off.* What I was doing—what I had been doing all my life—had failed. I was nothing. I wanted to . . . do nothing. There was nothing I *could* do. *He looks again at the cardinals.* Nothing *of that sort:* fishing for compliments, staking claims for honors and rewards, seeking fame and fortune, petitioning for favors, soliciting approvals, requesting confirmations, endorsements, permissions, licenses. . . . All on the assumption that you were my admiring schoolteachers, my smiling uncles and aunts, my adoring parents. Benign authority sits on the throne, and all I have to do is submit my proofs and practice my persuasions and there will follow that most indispensable boon: *recognition.* Only not any more. You have relieved me of that illusion along with others, and helped me to see you, not as my friends and allies and patrons, which you aren't, but as my enemies and nothing but my enemies, which you are. Enemies! Not just Scheiner. All of you master politicians! Including the nice ones who just walked out. And the sad one who sits in the Vatican, weeping for mankind, because he thinks our discoveries are too much for people, such terrible things are going to be discovered. But, my lords, since God made the universe, nothing can be discovered that He didn't put there. And since God is wise, He can't put there anything we ought not to discover. I find in our Holy Father a deep mistrust of our Heavenly Father. As if the Lord God needed the hierarchy of the Catholic Church to make up for His own insufficiency. You would go God one better, my lords. And so when I come along with the faculties He gave me and read some heretofore undeciphered words in the open book of His heaven, what do you have to say to me? "*Stop* reading." When you thus set bounds to the mind of man, do you not sense in your actions an affront to man's Maker?

CASTELLI. Galileo, take care!

GALILEO. Why? Why should I take care? For the first time in my life, I *want nothing* from the hierarchy of the Catholic Church. I am their enemy. And for an enemy there is only one question, that of strategy: how best to attack, when, where? Father Scheiner thinks I'm afraid to die. Wrong! Yesterday I *wanted* to be dead. Today I don't want to die, but if it is the best way to fight you, my lords, I will do it. And it *is* the best way because, as Scheiner explained, it is the only way. So I accept it. Gladly. And I can't tell you what a relief, what a joy, it is to shed at long last the servility and complaisance of life in this our Italy! Burn me! Yes! Burn me! The flames will be seen all the way to London!

Silence. But Scheiner is coming out of the state of shock the slap had put him into.

SCHEINER, *very quietly indeed.* The prisoner will return to his seat.

Castelli gets Galileo back to his seat and the two of them whisper excitedly while Scheiner addresses the tribunal as follows.

SCHEINER. My lords, we are confronted with a totally new situation.

CARDINAL 4. Yes, indeed. I move that we adjourn till tomorrow.

CARDINAL 5. First, he strikes Scheiner in the face! Next, he threatens to make a Protestant martyr of himself! I agree with Gorazio, let's adjourn!

SCHEINER. You take the change to be one for the worse, Cardinal Sordi.

CARDINAL 4. Certainly. How could it be for the better?

SCHEINER. A dead heretic is less dangerous than a live one.

CARDINAL 5, *amazed.* You mean we should take him up on it?

SCHEINER. You are the tribunal, my lords.

He is passing the ball to the Jesuit cardinals. They handle it in gingerly fashion at first.

CARDINAL 3. The prisoner is no longer young, of course. It is better if our enemies die of natural causes. . . .

SCHEINER. My information is that he has another book in his head. One that will be as subversive in mechanics as this other in astronomy.

CARDINAL 2. We shall have him under guard, of course. The Inquisition can take care that. . . .

SCHEINER. Alas, this is not the Spanish Inquisition. It is Italian, and therefore inefficient.

CARDINAL 1. Scheiner has a point there. A very big point. We all know what the experience has been, here in Italy, with writers under house arrest.

Galileo gestures to Castelli to stop talking and listen.

CARDINAL 4. What?

CARDINAL 1. They have been a thorn in the flesh.

CARDINAL 3. They have hangers-on, you see. Visitors. Admirers. Hardly surprising that their writings circulate in manuscript.

CARDINAL 2. The notoriety of such manuscripts sometimes gives them a wider circulation than books.

CARDINAL 1. In short, such imprisonment could be regarded as *desirable*. From the standpoint of a malcontent, I mean. As a spot to shoot from. A sniper's dream.

Galileo looks at Castelli. "Do you hear what I hear?" his eyes say.

CARDINAL 3. Some of them even get their stuff published. Abroad. Smuggled out to London and Leyden.

Galileo drops the scroll; Castelli retrieves it.

SCHEINER. And may I point out the special appeal the situation would have for Galileo Galilei? He gives us his authority to say the sun moves round the earth. But he has already taught his admirers not to believe anything on authority, including his. "The earth goes its way," he will be saying, *"and I go mine."*

CARDINAL 2. One might almost ask what good is such a recantation anyway? Our countrymen are apt to see *everything* as pretence.

CARDINAL 3. They'll certainly see through this.

CARDINAL 1. Then are we agreed that the death sentence must be reintroduced?

CARDINAL 4. I am still worried about another "martyrdom."

SCHEINER. It is a worry, if I may so, my lord, that can be dispelled.

CARDINAL 4. How?

SCHEINER. A burning need not be public. An execution need not be a burning.

CARDINAL 3. A *secret* execution could be arranged.

CARDINAL 2. Or simply a . . . disappearance.

CARDINAL 4. That would *certainly* head him off, wouldn't it?

CARDINAL 5. How exactly, um. . . . *He looks nervously across at Galileo and Castelli. Scheiner gets the point.*

SCHEINER. I might suggest, my lords. . . . *He leans forward to whisper to the five cardinals, who are now all in a huddle together around a table. Galileo and Castelli are watching them. All of a sudden without warning, Galileo walks to the center of the floor, and sinks to his knees.*

GALILEO, *intoning in Latin. Mea culpa, mea culpa, mea maxima culpa! Quia peccavi nimis cogitatione, verbo et opere! Mea culpa, mea culpa, mea maxima culpa. . . !*

The cardinals rise to their feet in consternation. Has the accused taken leave of his senses?

SCHEINER, *firmly, as to a hysterical child.* What's the matter, Galilei?

GALILEO, *stops intoning.* My guilt, my guilt, my guilt. . . .

SCHEINER, *as before.* What about your guilt?

GALILEO. I feel it now. Disobedience. Defiance. Encouragement of heresy. . . .

CARDINAL 5. He has turned around?

CARDINAL 4. Seen the light at last?

GALILEO, *intoning again. Confiteor! Deo omnipotenti, beatae Mariae semper Virgini, beato Michaeli Archangelo. . . .*

CARDINAL 1. Let's be clear about this. Are you agreeing to recant—in the words prescribed?

GALILEO. I am! I am!

CARDINAL 1. You know that you will be placed under house arrest for life?

GALILEO. I do! I do!

CARDINAL 1. And that your book is wiped from the record?

GALILEO. Oh yes! Yes!

Pause.

SCHEINER. He is putting on an act. The device is transparent.

CARDINAL 2. That's true. We can't let him get away with this.

CARDINAL 5. You are questioning the sincerity of a confession?

CARDINAL 4. The Inquisition's punishments are revocable upon confession of guilt. If we start questioning the sincerity of confessions, where will it end?

CARDINAL 3. If he *wants* to recant, we can't very well stop him. After all, it was our idea.

SCHEINER. But, my lord. . . .

CARDINAL 1. No, Scheiner. Bandolfi is right. Let things take their course.

SCHEINER. But the advantages of his position—

CARDINAL 1. The real advantages are always with those in power. Think back. This is a greater victory than we had any right to expect. The man will virtually be in prison for the rest of his days. What does it matter if we leave him free to wriggle and squirm a little? The sun will keep moving, and the earth will keep still, that's the thing. *Suddenly, as if he had been in charge all along.* The session is adjourned. *All begin to leave.* Give the prisoner his instructions, Scheiner.

SCHEINER, *coming out of a daze.* Huh? Oh yes, yes. *And he is soon alone with Galileo and Castelli.* Your escort will be here in a moment. The ceremony is set for next Tuesday in the Convent of Santa Maria Sopra Minerva. At twelve noon.
Scheiner leaves. A long silence.

CASTELLI. When you began to recite the *mea culpa* I thought for a second you'd gone stark staring mad.

GALILEO, *very slowly; he is drained of energy.* Scheiner knew better, didn't he?

CASTELLI. I'm just plain relieved. That you'll live, I mean. That you'll *not* be a martyr.

GALILEO. I wouldn't have been a *martyr* anyway.

CASTELLI. In God's eyes you might have been. Even killed in a dark alley. Murder is not hidden from Him.

GALILEO. I don't have a martyr's calling. Just lost control for a moment there. Their talk about the advantages of recantation and the possibilities of life under house arrest brought me to my senses.

CASTELLI. But, as Silotti explained, they exaggerated.

GALILEO. They offered something. Something far more real, far more *me,* than martyrdom. And maybe just as useful. What was Silotti's phrase?

CASTELLI. He feared you'd be "a thorn in the flesh."

GALILEO. Just what a good Catholic should be.

CASTELLI. You have always craved recognition—

GALILEO. I hereby abandon that morbid—no, that *naive*—craving. Let

DISCORSI
E
DIMOSTRAZIONI
MATEMATICHE,
intorno à due nuoue scienze

Attenenti alla

MECANICA & i MOVIMENTI LOCALI;

del Signor

GALILEO GALILEI LINCEO,

Filofofo e Matematico primario del Sereniſſimo
Grand Duca di Toſcana.

Con vna Appendice del centro di grauità d'alcuni Solidi.

IN LEIDA,
Appreſſo gli Elſevirii. M. D. C. XXXVIII.

Title page of *Two New Sciences,* "the book on motion," as published by the Elzevirs of Leyden, Holland, in 1638. The emblem shows (?) Galileo eating of the tree of knowledge, and the inscription reads *Non solus*—"not alone."

110

this be the real recantation. The world owes me nothing. *With a change of tone, almost to a "lighter vein."* But there's something I owe the world, Castelli. Can you be in Florence by tomorrow?

CASTELLI. You want me to go on ahead?

GALILEO. Get that second copy of my book. Take it to Van Gelder's.

CASTELLI. The Dutch merchant?

GALILEO. Have one of his people take it to the Elzevirs in Leyden.

CASTELLI. That's the publishers?

GALILEO. Then ride over to Virginia's convent. Break the news to her gently, and when she asks how I'm bearing up, say, quite well, considering, and that I've made a good resolution.

CASTELLI. Have you? Already? What is it?

GALILEO. My next book will be on a quite different subject.

CASTELLI. The book on motion? But *that's* going to be even more revolutionary.

GALILEO. Sh!

The clank of armor has been heard. It is the guard coming to take Galileo back to his quarters.

GUARD. Professor Galilei!

GALILEO, *preparing to leave. To Castelli.* Think of me next Tuesday at twelve noon.

CASTELLI. Will you be all right?

GALILEO, *with the shadow of a smile.* The earth won't have stopped moving.

Portrait of Galileo by Allan Ramsay, painted in 1757—one hundred and fifteen years after the scientist's death—and today in Trinity College, Cambridge. (*Bettmann Archive*)

Epilogue

June 22, 1633. In the great hall of the Convent of Santa Maria Sopra Minerva in Rome, a man in a penitential shirt is on his knees before the Congregation of the Holy Office. A Bible on the stone floor beside him, he reads from a scroll as follows:

I, GALILEO GALILEI, DO NOW, WITH A SINCERE HEART AND UNFEIGNED FAITH, ABJURE, DETEST, AND CURSE THE HERETICAL BELIEF THAT THE EARTH MOVES AROUND THE SUN, AND TAKE MY OATH THAT NEVER AGAIN WILL I SPEAK, WRITE, OR OTHERWISE ASSERT ANYTHING THAT MIGHT LEND PLAUSIBILITY TO THIS BELIEF. SHOULD ANYONE SUSPECTED OF SUBSCRIBING TO THIS HERETICAL BELIEF BE KNOWN TO ME, I SHALL DENOUNCE HIM TO THIS HOLY OFFICE IN ROME OR TO THE INQUISITOR IN WHATSOEVER PLACE I SHALL BE, SO HELP ME GOD AND THIS HOLY BOOK.

In 1638 the poet John Milton was in Florence. "There it was," he later wrote, "that I found and visited the famous Galileo, grown old, a prisoner of the Inquisition." This picture of Galileo and Milton is a detail from a painting by Annibale Gatti of around 1877. (*Bettmann Archive*)

AND 335 YEARS LATER Galileo Galilei made front page news in *The New York Times,* July 2, 1968.

Vatican May Lift Censure of Galileo

Special to The New York Times

BONN, July 1—Franz Cardinal König, Archbishop of Vienna, announced today that the Roman Catholic Church might revise its censure of Galileo Galilei, the 17th-century Italian scientist who was declared a heretic for asserting that the earth moves around the sun.

Pope Paul VI authorized Cardinal König to make the announcement at a meeting of Nobel Prize winners in Lindau, on Lake Constance, a spokesman for the church in Bonn said today.

More than 20 Nobel Prize winners were present when the Austrian Cardinal declared in his lecture on "Religion and Science" that the Vatican might institute a special commission to "retry" Galileo.

Galileo, who lived from 1564 until 1642, recanted his theory under threat of torture before the Inquisition in Rome in 1633. He had to spend the last years of his life in strict seclusion at a villa in Florence.

By 1616, consulting theologians of the Holy See had already condemned as heretical the theory first advanced by Copernicus in the 16th century that the sun is the center of the universe and that the earth performs a diurnal motion of rotation.

Cardinal König said that revision of the Galileo judgment "could heal one of the deepest wounds between religion and science." He did not say when the commission would start its work but he stressed that "steps to achieve a clear and open solution are already under way."

Cardinal König was the first churchman to address the traditional meeting of Nobel Prize winners.

The Cardinal said that the world was still being ruled by "bankers, generals and professional politicians" and that, now as before, "their practical intelligence" was in charge of "deadly arsenals." The scientists, as representatives of "modern intelligence," still did not have sufficient say in important matters, he added.

There was no reason, the Cardinal continued, why theologians who severed all links with political forces should not cooperate with "those scientists whose misgivings about political developments are generally known."

115

It is now over thirty years since a great many people both in Europe and America were reading a fictional biography of Galileo called *The Star Gazer*. Of the final crisis in Galileo's life as presented in this book, Henry Seidel Canby wrote in "The Book of the Month Club News":

His theses·proved, his fame spread through Europe, an oldish man, afraid of pain . . . he was broken by the Inquisition. He recanted shamelessly, dragging his belly on the ground before his potential torturers. He knew the earth moved, and that the skies were not immutable, but eagerly denied his knowledge to escape burning at the stake. . . . And at the end, it is the Inquisition itself that, by proclaiming his denials throughout the world, advertised their evident falsity.

Wasn't Galileo intelligent enough to *foresee* that such a proclamation would "advertise" the "evident falsity" of "his denials"? And, if he was, then must one not reconsider these accusations of shameless belly-dragging and craven fear of death? Eric Bentley does just this in his nine "Scenes from History Perhaps." The result is a new—or new old—interpretation of the whole Galileo story. Here Galileo is seen as the spoiled darling of an Establishment, his aim, until the crisis of 1633, nothing more nor less than to win that Establishment over to his view of the universe. Only when he definitively fails in this campaign does he rebel, and thus become a revolutionary in a social as well as a scientific sense: he will spend his last years in conscious conflict with the hierarchy, a smuggler of spiritual contraband. Even at this point, though, he is no nineteenth-century radical, denouncing Christianity and crying, "neither God nor master!" He is closer, rather, to some of the Catholic radicals of the twentieth century who, instead of challenging the church as such, challenge current office-holders and power-wielders. It was, however, much harder for this man to really recant his assumptions about the Establishment than to pretend to recant his assumptions about the universe.

72 73 74 75   12 11 10 9 8 7 6 5 4 3 2 1